REEL TO RATTLING REEL

STORIES AND POEMS ABOUT MEMORIES OF CINEMA-GOING

EDITED BY SARAH NEELY & NALINI PAUL

Jots of love
Kay x

cranachan

the projector being aimed at
a whiteish screen on its shoogly stand
was made ready to purr, when,
reel to rattling reel, the story was spun

Aonghas MacNeacail
remembering which film

CONTENTS

3 UNFORGETTABLE PEOPLE

4 MEMORABLE FILMS

5 GROWING UP WITH THE CINEMA

BIOGRAPHIES

Reel to Rattling Reel: Editors' Introductions

SARAH NEELY

This anthology arises from the project, *The Major Minor Cinema: The Highlands and Islands Film Guild*, a three-year collaborative research project between the University of Glasgow and the University of Stirling[1].

The project focuses on the history of the Highlands and Islands Film Guild, a mobile cinema service established in 1946 and in operation until the 1970s, which served many functions. It sought to address issues of depopulation through a general improvement of the cultural and recreational offerings in rural communities. It also served an educational function by working closely with local community associations and educational authorities to develop opportunities for using films as an educational tool in schools. It also aimed to encourage local film production.

Although *The Major Minor Cinema* is primarily an oral history project that has largely focused on gathering first-hand accounts of the Guild screenings in communities throughout the Highlands and Islands, the project also includes a creative writing strand which was developed in response to initial findings. Ian Goode,

[1] This project was made possible with funding from the Arts and Humanities Research Council (AHRC project grant AH/N001605/1).

1

who is leading the project, conducted an early pilot study in Orkney, and made a surprising discovery of a number of creative writing responses that audience members had written about their own experiences of going to the Guild screenings.

In response to these initial findings, the creative writing strand aims to explore the relationship between creativity and memories of cinema-going. A series of creative writing and storytelling workshops were held at various locations throughout the Highlands and Islands in order to stimulate creative responses in relation to the memories of cinema-going in rural communities. This strand of the project also included the creative writing competition which forms the basis for this anthology.

The competition was open to writers, writing in English, from around the world. For the competition's launch, five writers from the Highlands and Islands were commissioned to write creative works responding to their own memories of cinema-going: Christine De Luca (Shetland), Aonghas MacNeacail (Skye), Alison Miller (Orkney), Kevin McNeil (Lewis), and Christie Williamson (Shetland). The commissioned writers' contributions appear in this anthology alongside twenty works selected from the competition entries.

Although the publication was not intended to focus entirely on memories of the Highlands and Islands Film Guild, we were pleased to receive first-hand accounts from two of our commissioned writers, as well as a few competition entrants. Christine De Luca and Anne Huntley reflect on their memories of the Guild in Shetland in their work, while Aonghas MacNeacail's and Donald S Murray's contributions, draw from their memories of the Guild screenings in the Western Isles (Skye and Lewis respectively). There are also a number of accounts depicting many of the other forms of mobile and non-theatrical cinemas to have operated throughout rural Scotland over the years, such as David Sinclair and Richard Clubley's piece on the wartime cinemas established on the small Orkney island of Flotta (which served as an important military base), and the competition's winning entry, 'Big Dreams in a Wee Place', a story by Sam Gates, which draws from memories of cinema-going in the small villages of rural Ayrshire.

In addition to these entries, the publication that follows presents an exciting range of creative responses to the competition's open call for writers to reflect on memories of cinema-going. In some cases, writers draw from their own, individual memories. In other cases, the source of inspiration comes from the memories of friends or family members (for instance, Alison Miller's story draws from her mother's accounts of cinema-going written in her diary). Many of the contributions also brilliantly capture a sense of the collective forms of memory held in relation to cinema, which often focus

3

on popular films, film stars or key events that are likely
to have figured in the memories of many cinemagoers.

A number of the stories and poems contained within
this volume also draw from a similar set of thematic tropes
in their narrativisation of cinema memory. In particular,
many writers' accounts focus on the imaginative space
and sense of freedom which the cinema seemed to
provide for them, particularly during adolescence.
Although some of the contributions focus on the films
themselves, several make little or no mention of the film
at all. For many writers, the experience of going to the
flicks contained a multitude of novel experiences that
stretched beyond the actual film that they saw. Several
contributors gave considerable attention to the journeys
they made to and from the cinema. There was also a
marked interest in the actual space of the cinema – the
layout, where the projector was, where they sat, whom
they sat next to, etc. The sensory nature of going to the
cinema was also of interest – the sights and sounds, but
also the smells (both good and bad!), the tastes of the
sweets or popcorn they may have purchased or brought
along, and the bodily experience of sitting in the austere
surroundings of the village hall (the hard seats and
cold temperatures) in contrast to the more pleasurable
accounts of the luxurious surroundings of purpose-built
cinemas. Aonghas MacNeacail, whose poem provided
the title for this anthology – 'Reel to Rattling Reel' –

wonderfully captures the kind of sensory details of the cinema-going experience that feature in many of the contributions.

The structure of this anthology aims to highlight some of these key themes by presenting the work through thematic sections. Each section opens with the work of one of our commissioned writers, which is followed by writing selected from the competition entries which seems to respond to that particular theme. In many cases, there is overlap in the themes, with many contributions responding to several of the themes identified. However, it is hoped that structuring the individual contributions in this way will enable an appreciation of both their uniqueness and commonalities.

The writing presented in this anthology is the result of several years' work on behalf of a number of individuals and organisations. In addition to thanking the writers for their wonderful contributions, we'd also like to thank the various festivals who supported the project by helping to publicise the competition and/or hosting the various events and writing workshops. These include: Glasgow Short Film Festival, National Library of Scotland's Moving Image Archive (NLSMIA), Inverness Film Festival, Orkney Storytelling Festival, Shetland Screenplay and HebCelt Festival in Lewis. We are also extremely grateful for Cranachan's enthusiasm for the project and willingness to publish the work at such a late stage when we were left without a publisher following the demise of Freight Books. Finally, we'd like to give special thanks to Aonghas MacNeacail (and his poem) for providing the title for the anthology, and to Emily Munro at NLSMIA, who first selected it as the title for our event held at Glasgow Short Film Festival.

NALINI PAUL

Looking at memories of cinema-going in the Highlands and Islands has been inspiring for my own writing and resonates with my own experiences. In addition to members of the team interviewing the older generation who remember the Mobile Cinema, Sarah and I had the pleasure of travelling to Inverness, Lewis, Shetland and Orkney to deliver Creative Writing workshops with members of the public. Interestingly, participants were often not originally from the Highlands or Islands. As an 'incomer' myself, I found this encouraging. I was born in India, grew up in Canada, and have been living in Scotland for most of my adult life. Based in Orkney as George Mackay Brown Writing Fellow (2009-10), I felt welcome and included in every respect, and embraced island life for a year that I will never forget.

It was good to see that same outward-looking inclusivity amongst locals at our various ports of call, which seems to come from a strong sense of community and cultural identity. The latter is ever evolving, but in a stable and self-affirming way. Cinema is clearly one of the foundations of many people's memories, whether from Hungary, the United States, Canada or Mainland Scotland. Such was the geographic range of participants in the workshops.

Using memory, visual images and sensory recollections, participants produced a rich and varied offering at the workshops. Some were humorous, while others brought tears. All were honest and significant ways of engaging with the past. From the sweeties displayed behind glass at the cinema, to the plush, velvet seats in the auditorium, to the use of hot-water bottles at community hall screenings, the memories gathered make for quite the journey.

This inspired me to write a poem, which I hadn't 'planned' on writing, about my own cinematic memories. The images came to me as tastes, smells and sounds, as well as the strangely unreal/real quality that visual memories take on, years and miles away from their points of origin.

FAMOUS PLAYERS

Mid-summer, leaving the shopping-mall movie theatre, salted, buttered popcorn coats the tongue. Gummy bear jewels cling between teeth.

Dreams of lilac light wrap layers
around my cooling heart.
Coming out of the warm, chocolate-box
velvet-cushioned seats, where darkness

cradled me, was the comfort
of not-knowing,
the what-will-happen-next
that hovers in night air,
between your thoughts and who you were
yearning to be.

Remembering the heroine in pink: as real as your plastic
shoes and bracelet – visions alight and dissolve
like starbursts, crackling sugars in the mouth.

I walk across still-lit suburbia,
sidewalks smelling of residual heat.

The Skytrain whizzes past, the sun long set.
And we all feel a sense of our childhoods fading…

*Note: Famous Players was the leading chain of movie
theatres in Canada, which in 2005 was sold to Cineplex
Galaxy. The Skytrain is a form of rapid-transit public
transport, connecting Vancouver with surrounding cities.*

The pieces selected from the range of submissions offer richly textured worlds – old and new, real and imagined – in which to escape. Ailsa Thom's 'The Perfect Frame' charts the life of a projectionist as the world around him changes: patriotic black-and-white films, World War II, and the loss of his beloved Betty, sit poignantly alongside each other as the story moves us on. Roseanne Watt's poem, 'Mareel', gives us a moment of connection between two people, as they enter 'the cinema-dark of the evening' to see the aurora borealis: 'the dancers, unspooling/their reels of green across the sky'. There are also light-hearted pieces, including 'Gremlins II', a close-up of a panicked, under-aged girl who is terrified of being barred from her favourite film.

Our winning entry – a difficult decision, as there were some real gems here – was 'Big Dreams in a Wee Place' by Sam Gates. It draws on the innocence of childhood and the first encounters with cinema in a rural community, following the life of the unnamed main character and his pal, Andy, who dreams of becoming a projectionist. There is a sense of fascination with the new and magical world of cinema. When Technicolor arrives, the cinema becomes more real than life:

the blue cavalry uniforms, rust-coloured landscapes and braw sunsets that reminded him of the shades in his paintboax.

But it is the main character's singing voice that takes the story to unexpected heights, uniting the community, giving him a sense of purpose as his friend pursues his dream. And it is that strange, enthralling quality of cinema, its power to merge dreams with reality, which will – we hope – keep cinema alive for future generations.

Big Dreams in a Wee Place
SAM GATES
(Competition Winner)

He wis nearly eight and three-quarters when he saw his furst picture. Sorn wis jist a wee place; there wis nae picture hoose, and naeb'dy could bring a mobile cinema intae the village till efter the war, when petrol wis easier tae come by. Then wan day a notice went up in the paper shoap windae:

PICTURE SHOW

SATURDAY 30ᵀᴴ SEPTEMBER
7PM
CONSTITUTIONAL HALL
SORN
Adults 6d /Children 3d

As the news buzzed roon the village, mair and mair folk said they were gaun – but no' him. His three big sisters had been tae the pictures in Kilmarnock, and he heard them saying something he didnae like – something that made him think aboot his secret.

His mither talked aboot the pictures tae; she wis helping him read *Treasure Island* that week and mentioned it had been made intae a film wae actors,

11

costumes and big sailing ships. He swithered. He had sometimes tried tae imagine the pictures in his book coming tae life, but he wisnae sure he could go tae a real picture show. His pal Andy would be there – he would wait and hear whit he said aboot it.

The mornin' efter the show Andy chapped the door, anxious tae blurt oot the news: he had been ootside the Constitutional Hall when a swanky big Austin Sixteen drew up; oot came the Picture Man, a projector, a screen, hauf a dozen reels and a big wummin tae collect the dosh. They were fae Muirkirk, but that wis tolerated because they put oan a smashin' show for the Sorn crowd. There wis mair: the man had a big stock of cowboy pictures, and the titles for next week were *Silver Spurs* and *Outlaws of the Cherokee Trail*. Listenin' tae Andy made him feel excited and feart at the same time. Outlaws and Cherokees galloped roon his heid a' week till he wis in a right fankle, but eventually – oan the Saturday mornin' – he asked his mither if she would take him tae the pictures that night.

Doon the hall, he had never seen that mony folk thegither in wan place, and he huddled close tae his mither. He kept askin' her when the lights were gaun oot, and when it suddenly happened she grabbed his haun. He keeked roon tae make sure naeb'dy had noticed, and saw – in an eerie light – the happy, excited faces of his neebors and pals. Then, when he turned back and looked at the screen, he wis loast in anither world.

He would never forget thon night he saw his furst moving images, watched his furst actors, heard his furst movie soundtrack; the night he discovered the magic screen that flickered intae life and helped him face his secret fear – the daurk.

Andy became his picture buddy, and every Seturday they hit the trail for the Constitutional Hall thegither. Andy wis three year aulder than him; his faimly were originally evacuees fae Glesga, but they were fair ta'en wae the wee village that ran alangside the River Ayr, and managed tae stay oan efter the war. Andy missed the Glesga cinemas; his Big Dream wis tae become a projectionist, and his furst target wis tae buy his ain projector, so he delivered the papers, put his wages intae the Post Office and hid the book in an auld shoe under his bed. Andy jumped oan the weekly bus tae Glesga every Seturday mornin'; he went up tae visit an uncle who took him tae learn aboot cameras and projectors at the Amateur Film Society – but he wis aye back in time tae catch the cowboys wae his wee sidekick.

The boays liked tae be furst doon the hall, when their voices sounded big in the empty space and the chairs were lined up tae perfection, waiting for the pictures tae stert. Andy would help the Picture Man unload his equipment and set it up as the big folk arrived for their cups a tea in the Lesser Hall, then a posse of weans would breenge in and race tae claim a seat in the front row. When the big folk had dribbled intae the main hall the man would flick oan his projector lamp tae show it wis time; someb'dy would cry, 'shoosh!' and everything happened at once – the lights went oot, the music sterted and the cheers ran roon the hall: *Yippee-yi-ay! Send for the Cavalry! Wagons ho!*

Week efter week, cowboys and Indians slugged it oot doon the hall. He described every picture tae his faither, who couldnae go oan Seturday nights because he had tae attend special meetings in the Greyhound Inn.

Sorn wis too wee tae have cubs or a fitba' team and he wondered whit he would dae if there were nae cowboy pictures. Sometimes, in the long wait fae wan Seturday tae the next, he acted oot his ain movie scenes: he would imagine his bogie wis a covered wagon and sneak aff tae Timmer's Brig, where the burn became a creek and he wis a cavalry scout planning a raid oan Indian territory – or a Navajo brave charging up the bank oan a pony withoot a saddle and taking cover tae watch the movements of the Paleface doon the village.

The hall wis hoachin' every Seturday, so the weans were sent tae sit oan the flair doon the front, and eventually the Picture Man started anither weekly show: *Friday at the Flicks.* That suited Andy – he wis taking turns at the projector noo and wis sometimes left in charge when the man went ootside for a quick smoke.

The pictures seeped intae village life. He and his pals skooshed wan anither wae Flash Gordon watter pistols. Lassies skipped aboot singing 'Aa've got legs like Betty Grable'. Shiny copies of *Picturegoer* were passed roon the hooses. His sisters swapped cigarette cards of movie stars. Some folk went tae the pictures three and four times a week: wee gaggles of folk traipsed a mile up the road tae catch a bus for Auchinleck Picture Hoose while his sisters nipped up the ferm road tae the Wilson Hall in Catrine – they claimed it had a bigger screen than Sorn, but his faither said they jist went there tae ogle the Catrine mill boays.

When he wis big enough he wis allowed tae go tae Catrine wae Andy and his sisters tae see his furst Roy Rogers picture. He wisnae happy aboot sitting wae a crowd of strangers, and felt cheated when the famous cowboy appeared: he wis oan a fine wee cuddy, but wearin' a spangly shurt, fancy boots and stripey troosers! He decided Roy Rogers wisnae a real cowboy, but wis impressed when the man sterted tae sing: he seemed tae cast a spell ower the hall wae his saft, gentle voice and guitar. Then a wonderful thing happened: slowly … quietly … the audience jined in. He had never heard a crowd of folk sharing a song wae each ither like that; somethin' moved inside him, and he felt a smile breaking ower his face.

It wis daurk when they came oot – but he wisnae feart; the stars were oot and the moon showed them the road back tae Sorn. They slowed doon tae enjoy the waarm night, and he sterted tae hum the Roy Rogers song, till Andy asked him tae sing up:

Oh give me land, lots of land under starry skies above,
Don't fence me in …

The ithers helped him remember the words, and they sang their way back tae Sorn. They sat oan the brig for ages, looking at the stars and sharing stories fae their favourite pictures; naeb'dy waanted tae go in the hoose that night.

When the singing teacher telt him he could haud a guid tune, he began tae pay mair attention tae the music he heard at the pictures and decided tae stert a collection of cowboy songs; he and his faither copied doon the words aff the wireless and he kept them in a shoeboax oan tap of the wardrobe. The day he turned ten, his sisters gave him his furst three gramophone records, each by a different singin' cowboy – Gene Autry, Tex Ritter and Rex Allen. Efter his tea and cake, his mither telt him tae polish his guid shoes and comb his hair – they were headin' roon tae Andy's for 'a wee soirée and a big surprise'. He wisnae expecting this, and when they got tae Andy's, there – waiting oan the living room table – wis a film projector! Andy had saved up hauf the money and his uncle chipped in the rest.

A sheet wis rigged up oan the wa', and he felt a rush of pride as his pal loaded the furst reel intae his very ain projector. He listened tae the trig wee machine gaun *purrrrrr* and watched the bare film runnin' smoothly fae wan spool tae the ither till the pictures came up. Andy had hired twa films fae the Society in Glesga: wan aboot the Clyde steamers and anither called *Glimpses of Ayrshire* showin' places like the Brig o' Doon. They were silent pictures, so the big folk talked oot loud and shared their stories of trips oan the steamers before the war and the creepy auld kirk where Tam O'Shanter saw the deevil playing the bagpipes.

When the pictures feenished he wis asked tae gie the company a song, and his faither suggested *The Streets of Laredo*. He sterted aff, remembering the singing teacher's instructions: 'Take deep breaths, aim for the high notes and always tell the story.' Near the end he noticed Andy's mither had a wee greet, but she dabbed her eyes wae a hankie and said his singin' wis '*beautiful*'. Aye, it had been a guid birthday – and a guid night for Andy: his pal had sterted tae make his Big Dream come true.

The next summer, the talk in Sorn wis aboot the new Abbey Cinema in Mauchline. Andy heard they were showing a John Wayne picture, and inveigled him intae taking their bikes ower there tae see it. When he saw the poster ootside the cinema he understood why Andy wis keen: it wis in Technicolor! They went inside. The place wis painted gold, like a palace, wae a balcony and saft, jined-up seats – and as Andy pointed oot, there wis even a special wee room for the projector. He noticed a soor smell, but that seemed tae disappear when the lights went aff and the giant red curtains drew back; he gawked at the size of the screen – and jumped when the music sterted up. *He wis in an actual cinema, aboot tae watch his furst Technicolor movie …*

They had tae sit through a newsreel, cartoons, trailers, a serial and a wee picture before it wis time for the big attraction; by this time they had scoffed their sweeties, but at last, oan it came – *She Wore a Yellow Ribbon*. It wis a stoater. There were chases, fights, a stampede, real Cheyenne actors, and for the very furst time he could see everything in colour – the blue cavalry uniforms, rust-coloured landscapes and braw sunsets that reminded him of the shades in his paintboax. He cheered, laughed and gret wae the rest of the audience, and decided there wis only wan thing he could tell his faither aboot this picture: that he had tae see it for himsel'.

The picture feenished wae a song aboot 'the U.S. Caval-ree', and the crowd took the jaunty wee tune intae the street. But he didnae jine in the singin' – he had this queer, uneasy feeling in his heid. Andy said it wis because they had been sittin' in the daurk for nearly four hours – but he wis wrang.

That Seturday it wis back tae rickety widden chairs and black-and-white cowboys at the Constitutional Hall. They watched an auld film and a new wan jist as they had for years, but when they came oot and went for a pow-wow oan the brig, it wis *She Wore a Yellow Ribbon* they talked aboot.

Thon wis a strange summer. It wis nearly time for him tae leave Sorn primary and jine the big school while Andy wis beginning his apprenticeship as an electrician, hoping tae train as a projectionist when it feenished. He wis pleased for Andy, but worried in case he didnae see as much of him. How could things no stay the same? How would he like the big school? How come *he* didnae have a Big Dream like Andy? He wis scunnered. Then his teacher asked him tae sing a solo at the school prize-giving, so he lifted doon his shoeboax and went through his collection. He wis drawn tae an auld Gene Autry song, *Tumblin' Tumbleweeds*, aboot a wanderin' cowboy oan a lonesome trail; it haunted him for days, so it wis easy tae memorise.

As he stood oan the stage he could see the faces of weans, teachers, mithers, faithers and grannies looking up at him. By the end of his furst line a hush had settled oan the hall, but he stayed in control, watching his speed and keeping his voice low tae draw his audience in.

There wis silence as his last notes hung in the air, then somebody sterted tae clap; slowly the ithers jined in, then they cheered and whistled till he felt like Frankie Laine! The heidmaister came ower, grabbed his haun and telt him his singing wis a special gift, and he should use it tae bring pleisure tae ithers; he even asked him if he would come back next year and sing again, so when the bell went for the holidays he knew he wisnae leavin' for guid. He daunered hame, smiling – and thinking aboot the heidmaister's words.

The day he tried oan his furst long troosers, he felt he wis moving oan in life. The Picture Man wis moving oan tae: wae three programme changes a week, the Mauchline cinema wis a magnet for Sorn folk. The final film at the Constitutional Hall wis *The Last Trail*, a Tom Mix comedy – but the laughs didnae sound the same when the hall wis nearly empty. Efter the show, the twa pals helped the Picture Man load his equipment intae the big Austin and watched it disappear up the Muirkirk road for the last time. He didnae say oanything in case he burst oot greetin'.

They went tae sit oan the brig. Andy wisnae sayin' much either, so he left him tae nurse his thochts. As he listened tae the watter running by, he minded how the pictures had come intae the village, brocht everybody thegither and left each of them wae their ain memories.

20

He thocht aboot how their nights at the hall had opened up anither world tae him and his pal, a world that would aye be theirs – a world of fun, adventure, magic … and dreams.

This story has been based oan faimly memories. Names have been changed; oany resemblance tae real people – living or deid – is coincidental.

1

AT
THE
THRESHOLD

The Cinema Inside, The Cinema Outside
KEVIN MACNEIL

Jenny's idea is to shoot them as they go in and again when they come out.

She's brought a hand-held camera that looks and feels like a toy, but films to professional standard. She has a list of questions.

It's a dreich Wednesday afternoon. She shelters under the awning at her local cinema, a liminal space. This cinema transported her to other times, other lives – other planets, even. It's the cinema that inspired her to go to film school. This building taught her she has an infinite cinema inside her. She believes it's one of life's most valuable gifts, the imagination.

She looks up the drizzling street, wondering who, if anyone, will come to the cinema today. She used to make her way here as often as she could, loved escaping the small-town rain and grey routine.

She has made a couple of documentaries, but her ambition is to write and direct a feature-length drama. Meanwhile, the benefit of documentaries is that the people in front of the camera also provide character, dialogue and, to a certain extent, theme and plot. 'Drama,' said Hitchcock, 'is life with the dull bits cut out.'

An elegant woman of about seventy drifts up the

street towards the cinema and is only too pleased to be interviewed. 'Of course, darling,' she says with a confidence that makes Jenny realise the woman expects to be recognised.

'BBC, is it?' the woman asks, tidying strands of silver hair under a suave red hat.

Jenny blushes. 'Er, no, it's a documentary for a website I run, all about cinema.'

The woman nods and smiles and Jenny tries to place her as she asks about her cinema-going memories. Instead of answering directly, the woman talks of films and plays she has been in and Jenny understands the woman is indeed an actress and in fact is fairly well known. The woman says that as a schoolgirl she stayed in a hostel in Stornoway which overlooked the Playhouse cinema, a wonderful art deco building, and she and her friends would scrutinise the cinema entrance on Saturday evenings to see who was escorting their teachers to 'the flicks', then they would let their giggling imaginations run rampant.

Jenny looks at the woman's sculpted bone structure and her mind makes an automatic smash-cut, picturing her as a lively, pretty girl, with a relatively easy, glamorous life ahead of her. I wonder, thinks Jenny, if she was born for the role of actress.

The dignified woman talks of her stage and screen roles with nostalgia and vitality. 'The only regret I have, *a ghràidh*, is that more of the films I saw and played in weren't about The Highlands. There were some, but not enough, nowhere near enough. How are we supposed to pass on to the next generations who they are and where they come from, instead of showing them explosions and violence and Hollywood all the time?'

Jenny nods ruefully and asks if she'll give her a couple of moments of her time after the film for what is essentially the second part of the interview.

'Of course, *a ghràidh*,' says the woman and before entering the cinema she surprises Jenny by air-kissing her on each air-cheek.

The woman glides graciously into the cinema as if she herself will star in the film, or as if she is constantly acting in the film of her life.

Hand-in-hand, a couple in their late teens or early twenties saunters up the road, talking closely and laughing, taking up most of the pavement, oblivious to the drizzle, exuding a timeless joy as if delighted by the mere fact of being in each other's company. They're dressed in stylishly shabby clothes – Bohemian chic – and must be, by Jenny's reckoning, students in love.

When she asks them for an interview, they look at one another as if seeking permission before answering.

'Sure, why not,' says the male in a drawl.

In response to her question about their cinema-going memories, the answer is a list: *Star Wars, Harry Potter, Lord of the Rings*. Jenny asks about their favourite cinematic memory and they pause then burst out laughing at the same time, giving each other mischievous, almost sly, glances.

'What are you expecting from this film?'

'More great memories,' says the boy, grinning. He looks serious for a moment. 'Actually, I carry a cinema in my pocket,' he says, whipping a mobile phone out of his jacket. 'We're living in the future.'

No, Jenny thinks, you carry a better cinema in your head.

'We gotta go,' he says as he puts an arm around his girlfriend, already guiding her towards the entrance.

This interview, thinks Jenny, has been a dud.

As they're going through the door, the girl looks over her shoulder and calls back, 'No, wait - my favourite memory was seeing *It's a Wonderful Life* with my late father.'

But Jenny has already put the camera on pause.

She un-pauses it as a man about her own age approaches with an air of intensity. He is dressed in black and wears a goatee, a pork pie hat and thick-rimmed glasses.

He's happy to be interviewed, indeed looks comfortable in front of the camera. He quickly lets her know he is a trainee film director and he reels off a list of movies he loves: *Casablanca, Elephant, Ringu, Wild Strawberries, Brief Encounter*, and many others.

'Cinema,' he says, 'is all about dreaming other people's dreams, living other people's mistakes and victories and learning from them. When we were kids, we'd go and watch a film, then re-live it in the playground. You know, like recounting scenes from, I don't know, the *Airplane* films, or *The Empire Strikes Back*, or something. And so, cinema developed our storytelling skills, our performance skills, and it reinforced our sense of humour and our bonds of friendship. Even now I sometimes go to the cinema with a friend and watching a movie is, it's like we're sharing a book simultaneously.'

Jenny recognises in him a creativity, an ambition and an authenticity that she feels deep within herself. She'd like to watch a film with him, share popcorn and ideas and... more.

He describes a time he went to a film festival and 'watched' a film with no images whatsoever, just sound, it was an HP Lovecraft story, and afterwards he realised he'd essentially paid to hear an audiobook in a darkened public room.

His voice rises passionately as he talks of wanting to make a majestic film about Scottish music like the Sigur Rós documentary.

Jenny enjoys listening to him. He is now talking about subtext in dialogue and is writing his email address down for her.

She feels a bit tongue-tied and when he turns to go into the cinema it is all she can do not to slip her arm round his and accompany him in.

One more cinema-goer arrives, a thirtysomething Japanese man dressed in simple clothes that nonetheless look distinguished as they seem tailored to his wiry body. He walks in a manner that is at once relaxed and alert. He tells her his name is Kenji. He speaks very good English and his eyes smile constantly. His manner is measured, aware, serene. He pauses for a moment before answering each question.

'I like cinema because it has a lot to teach us about reality,' he says, looking at Jenny with a steady gaze. 'The images on the screen are neither in it nor out of it, like the reflection of the moon on the water.' This gives Jenny a pleasant intellectual jolt and to gain time to reflect she asks a simple question about his favourite films (which are *Late Spring*, *The Only Son* and *Spring, Summer, Autumn, Winter... and Spring*).

He's speaking again with that calm authority. 'I like being reminded that reality is, itself, an illusion, being ephemeral, like a bubble or dream or a flash of lightning. Reality is always changing, it's just that we believe its illusion of constancy, like we do when watching a film. And so what we think, we become.'

Jenny is not sure she follows what he is saying; it seems a non-sequitur. But she knows what he's saying will be good for the doc.

'I like that a person who isn't really there appears on the screen, pretending to be someone else, saying artificial words in an invented narrative. It makes you humble.'

Humble? thinks Jenny. She usually feels energised and emotionally enlarged by a visit to the cinema, not humbled.

'Okay?' he says.

'Okay,' she replies, a little perplexed.

He bows his head slightly, smiles, and moves out of shot, leaving Jenny staring into a lens that has defocused into grey rain and unreadable bright shop signs but she realises it is just her eyes; Kenji's words have left her staring into mid-air.

*

Inside the cinema, the older woman takes her seat and instead of looking at the screen she tilts her head back as she always does and gazes up at the cinema's distinctive ceiling, which she thinks of as 'the interior heavens', being a deliberate constellation of twinkling lights. It makes her swoon with thoughts of stars, time, destiny. Age.

While the adverts clamour, the students watch a YouTube video on his phone, idly crunching on popcorn, giggling. They treat the cinema not like a public space but a private one. The near-dark is like a duvet around them.

The aspiring director also takes his phone out. He checks his emails. Nothing. In truth, it was loneliness, not a desire to see the film, that brought him to the cinema today.

He thinks about action and consequence, how screenplays must always be karmic, and he wonders whether life might also truly work along those principles. He is desperate to know more about the woman who filmed him, and he mentally kicks himself for neglecting to ask her name. He worries he talked too much and came across as self-involved or even narcissistic. He resolves to do better when she interviews him afterwards. She had better be there. With no real information to go on, Google isn't helping him learn anything about her. At the very least, he wants to befriend her. She had sad, yearning eyes that spoke of authenticity and creativity.

Kenji watches the other cinemagoers in the glare and blare of the film trailers and adverts. He observes that the two individuals and the couple are each bound up in their thoughts and desires like a silk-worm in its cocoon.

The lights fade out and after a few deliciously crackling moments the screen fills with light, fills everyone's eyes with light.

*

Jenny did not watch the movie, deliberately so. For the next part of her project she moves into the foyer and waits until the scattered audience begins to leave the auditorium. She sets up her camera, planning to say to each person: 'Tell me about the film.'

The older woman with the lovely cheekbones looks as though she has been weeping. 'Oh, *a ghràidh*,' she says, 'it was just beautiful. Heart wrenching. I cried three times. I feel I've been put through the emotional wringer. It really spoke to me about my own youth and certain experiences I had as an actress on the stage. It moved me the way Shakespeare does.' She looks away and dabs her eyes with a handkerchief. 'You'll have to excuse me now,' she says, 'I'm going across the road for a brandy.' She smiles one last time at the camera and briefly puts her slender hand around Jenny's wrist and gives an affectionate squeeze. She brushes away Jenny's thanks and glides out the door, making for the bar across the street.

Jenny asks the students if she can interview them separately. They agree.

The boy says of the film, 'I don't know.' He grins and offers a misjudged wink. 'I didn't see all of it. I was too involved in, uh, eating the popcorn and, uh, other sweet treats.' Then, off Jenny's look, he says, 'But no, the film was tense and fast and exciting. I really liked it, especially the soundtrack. I realised that when the music speeds up, so does your heartbeat…' His voice trails off. He shakes his head. 'Yeah, I don't know – ask her,' he says, pointing.

So Jenny does. And, as she expected, the female student is more interesting than her boyfriend. 'It really made me think,' she says. 'At times I was scared that I was, you know, vicariously living someone else's darker instincts. Then I wondered whether that's not, at least on some level, cathartic. I'll have to think about it more. And as for the scene in the tunnel – well, that's tonight's nightmare taken care of, right?' She laughs nervously.

The students retrieve each other's hand and exit as one, in search of pizza. Jenny notices a tightness in her throat as she asks the film director to stand a little to the side. The light catches his features perfectly.

His take on the film is that it was, 'A wonderful amalgam of the conventional and the unexpected. I mean, all Western narratives pretty much follow the same structure of ordinary world, extraordinary world, complications, climax and resolution, but this one did so with real… panache… But… but I have to say, I was a bit distracted. It wasn't so much the film that inspired me – can we, can we turn the camera off for a moment? I'll give you a proper interview afterwards.'

As per her training, Jenny *pretends* to turn the camera off.

This is how she will always have a record of the time Jake nervously, but sweetly, asked her out on a date, and she accepted without having to think about it, and they made their way to the tapas place on the corner, and so happy-surprised was she that she forgot about the other interviewee, the Japanese guy, who must, in her mind, have thought her the single rudest human being in Scotland. She and Jake had so much to talk about. It was only when she was taking her first sip of red that she remembered and she blanched, swore and said, ''Scuse me a second,' and bolted out the restaurant and ran to the cinema, but of course the Japanese man, Kenji, was gone.

Kenji is fine. Nothing perturbs him. Whereas the others had emerged from the cinema blinking as they came back to 'the real world', he knew he was only moving from one sense of reality to another. He stepped into the street scene – a cold damp evening brimming with chatter and traffic noises – and he was perfectly at home in a foreign country, fully aware that the film of 'reality' refreshes itself quicker than the human eye can see, maintaining its illusion, empty and ungraspable, ever changing, all things to all people.

Millimetre by Millimetre
ELEANOR CAPALDI

The blue velvet drapes parted and the house lights dimmed for the third time that day. Sophie had always loved the hug of the dark, and the many viewings which embedded these films in her memory. Unlike the ones she watched at home by herself, eyes split between various screens, stories quickly forgotten. Here, there was only one to focus on.

Tickets taken, and with a careful eye on the customers, she took up her place on the usher's seat. Tucked in the corner, dressed all in black, she was indistinguishable from her surroundings. Like an excellent waiter, she knew the job was being done well if everyone forgot she was there. The guidance rating disappeared and the opening credits rolled. Flickering cracks scattered across the screen almost immediately. Thirty-five millimetre reels were currently whirring through the projector, brought out especially for today: Silver Screen Saturday. This matinee meant old favourites, lovingly re-watched, if not restored. Gradations of grey spun themselves into shadowy forms, as cads and dames began navigating their storylines.

The images abruptly became skewed, and slightly off kilter, before jumping downward. The top of the frame was slipping, now marked by a black line a quarter of the way down the screen. The characters' feet were walking along the top. A few audience members shuffled, and somebody's bag of hard-boiled sweets fell off their lap with a crumple. Half-head turns were angled in her direction. This wasn't so unusual with older projection methods, but everything ran so uniformly on the digital system, even the smallest slip could make it seem like the afternoon might be over too soon.

Sophie tapped on the projection booth door, quickly peering in through the small window to see a note on a scrap of paper beside the projector: 'Back in 5 minutes', it read. She sighed. Normally you couldn't shift the projectionist from their post. Of all the days, they'd abandoned it now. She'd been here long enough to have picked up a thing or two, though. And they did show her round the booth on her first day. Six years ago. She opened the door firmly.

The strip of film was passing through, unfolding with the story. She adjusted its position and peeked out the window onto the auditorium. The top of the frame aligned with the cinema screen once again. Feet now walked on the ground instead of on heads. Watching the movie, secluded, at once farther and closer to it, she began to imagine what she would say to the actors. How they could move, and where they would go, how they delivered their lines. A bit more of this, a bit less of that. Sophie's hand waved in front of her as she guided long-gone actors whose frozen reflections seemed to move in response.

Prising open a compartment of the projector where film that had been shown was resting, she released it, the film spooling in a heap at her feet. Bending down, she picked up a loose end, dangling it from her hands to the floor like a ladder. The booth had become a home for lost objects, and searching through it she came across old programmes, sellotape and a library card that belonged to an old member of staff. Then she found what she was after.

Holding the film negative up to the nearest light, it slowly came to life. Eyes narrowing and focusing, she raised the scissors and began to carefully cut around the outlines of the characters. With a miniature leading character in each hand, she raised them in front of the projection light. It shone brightly around them, throwing silhouettes on top of their big-screen counterparts. Rendered shadow puppets with slightly rough edges, they performed as she wanted them to. Reaching from the tops of her hands, they shrank and grew, dancing away from and towards each other as she orchestrated their movements. Though the audience couldn't hear what the silhouettes were saying from their static mouths.

She was so engrossed that all she could hear were the Boston-accented, fast-talking voices of the actors on the screen, and her own competing whispers. To her, the voices belonging to the shadows surfacing from underneath the booth door were silent.

Aids Film Paris, The Eighties
PATRICIA MCCAW

I decide on a rear-view row and inch past another woman
keeping shy of the long pins piercing her fierce grey bun.

Seats in front begin to fill as the lights fade, my neighbour
refuses to move up when late-comers tiptoe in.

A man slim as a sapling sits next to me, his jumper yellow
with puffy sleeves, white trainers brilliant in the gloom.

He pulls out knitting, watching the screen—slow purl, plain.
The Witnesses begins, its glow golden, as if a relic.

The cinema's wall echoes tonight's busy Edinburgh ambulances.
No breath to be heard, only needles hammering clickety click.

Gremlins II
KIRSTY ROWLEY

I was standing in the crowded foyer of my local cinema. My palms were sweating and I clutched some coins for dear life. My nemesis was in the vicinity, a towering inferno of pure evil. I tried my best to blend in. If I couldn't be seen, I couldn't be questioned. My main problem was that I had never been any use at lying. My second problem was that I knew it.

The seconds ticked slowly; we were all here for the same thing, of that there was no question. As I progressed to the front of the queue my breath quickened. I had her in my sights and, so far, I had remained undetected.

The noise of excited cinema goers echoed in my ears, the ring of the register and the chop chop of the guillotine-like ticket dispenser. My head was filled with the aroma of sweet, sweet popcorn with just a hint of nervous energy. Could it be coming from me?

My acting skills had never been through such a test, such a vitally important drill that I had practised at length in my bedroom until I was sick of the sound of my own voice.

She surveyed her prey contemptuously, nostrils flaring, eyes glaring. She gave a snort; a small puff of smoke exhaled and floated toward the ceiling. I was getting ever closer to her, inch by inch, millimetre by millimetre, willing her to look away.

Resplendent in head-to-toe black nylon, with a white frilly blouse and a gigantic grey blonde beehive, she was my worst nightmare, *this* was my worst nightmare.

As I came to be second in the queue we had an unspoken connection. I knew I was here to see Gremlins II, she knew I was here to watch Gremlins II and I knew she knew I was here to see Gremlins II. We both knew Gremlins II was a 12, but only I knew that I was 11.

Her job could be seen as a simple one. Her job was to challenge the age of her patrons. And challenge she did. It just so happened that this job could also ruin an 11-year-old's Saturday, their week, their month, their year. The year was 1990 and this was the most anticipated film of the year. This film could make or break an 11-year-old's playground reputation.

Finally my chance had come, I was facing the gatekeeper. This was a classic tale of good versus evil. I had one chance and one chance only to get this right. My preparation had been thorough, my adrenalin was in hyper-drive and most importantly my mum had said it was ok.

The time had come to face my demon. She turned, I steeled myself. She looked over my head, refocussed her slit-like eyes, tilted her head and looked down into my soul. I shifted my weight, suddenly aware of her red talons that were close enough to my throat to do some damage.

Her voice was other-worldly, time slowed down as she growled, "How old are you?"

I spoke immediately, quickly and as I had prepared in my training. "Eleven". Time stopped completely and my own squeaky voice rang in my ears.

Now she knew and I knew that I was not going to see Gremlins II today. I ran. I ran as fast as my legs could carry me back to my mum's blue Fiesta, parked in Safeway's car park next door where she had been waiting in case something went wrong.

The following weekend was much less dramatic. My mum took me to see Gremlins II and nobody batted an eyelid.

Mareel
ROSEANNE WATT

for Cara

Mind that night in November, the pair of us
bursting from Mareel like late-comers
to the cinema-dark of the evening.
How we nearly missed it, the other show

that night: the aurora, the dancers, unspooling
their reels of green across the sky, despite

a bone-bright moon in the south. Mind
how the waves in Hay's Dock lit up with this
borrowed phosphorescence, and we skirled

at the spectacle of it all; a sky of light, a sea of sky,
and behind us, the noost of Mareel,
its north-pointed prow.

2

INSIDE
THE
CINEMA

Catch
CHRISTIE WILLIAMSON

Siller dances apö da sun
free flowin laek a risin
tide fat wi mackerel

frish laek da drift
hurlin Nort Atlantik
chills an fugs skywards.

Sauchiehall Street nivvir saa
sic a exotic flock o birds
as caaed an cooried on da Foula cliffs.

Ilka line ivvir slippit
maun hae lures an bait an huiks.
Some bait is taestier as iddirs.
Some huiks nivvir laive your moo.

Here's aniddir catch
ta haal ahsore. Wast o dis
lies ony gold.

Ken Wast Yell?
CHRISTIE WILLIAMSON

Soond - tick - Yell tae da wastird
tides runnin laek da wirkins
o a clock at meezhirs mair
time as ee pair o lungs could respire.

Hoose lichts - tick - up fur da pilgrims
tae parade, awppin palms
touchin da cash box square
dan flicked aff fur da feature ta roll.

Print - tick - program decided
bi fair votes, practicalities
da package takkin pride o pliss
i da stentit Friday moarneen overland.

Sang - tick - Carla's ringin bittersweet
in hungry lugs afore da rods
dispersed wis tae da simmir dim
nesiks dancin tae da music o solidarity.

Recline
CHRISTIE WILLIAMSON

Eftir da mysteries
o da Bon Accord Grill
wis bön weel an truly
digested, nae navigation

wid be complete less a bellyfu
o St Clair air, aa da wye fae A deck
tae bolted portholes.
As broadcasts fizzed an foondird

wi da starnwird soup
atween wis an Bressay
ony celluloid guaranteed da murder
o hunders o meenits.

Da scale o da sea we pitched apö
wis onythin but minor. Aa at sank
wis da ivories dat nicht, but under
synthetic duvet waves

music dreamed o howldin a ocean
in hir airms. Da dance o da moarn's
brakkfist bell wis waetin aff da harbour,
da captains voice in tune wi da surf
kyissin aniddir day tae life.

Capturing Cinematic Memories
CHRISTIE WILLIAMSON

When I was invited to contribute to this project capturing cinematic memories of the Highlands and Islands, I was overjoyed. I love film, and completed an undergraduate degree at the University of Stirling as my first serious venture beyond Shetland.

Approaching the composition of the poems, I realised that by accepting the commission I was seriously challenging myself. I was born in Lerwick in 1976 and lived in Yell until I went to the Anderson High School in the early 1990s. Memories of life in Shetland have been a popular plunder of mine as a poet. Living in an island community you often have to compromise, to make do with not having things which are taken for granted elsewhere.

For most of my life in Shetland, one of the things we had to make do without was a cinema. Happily, this is something the next generation of Shetlanders cannot say but it has forced me to improvise a little in constructing these poems (no bad thing if you ask me).

'Catch' springs from a day of screenings and talks including Michael Powell's Edge of the World and Nort Atlantik Drift, Susan Kemp's exceptional film portrait of Robert Alan Jamieson. Glasgow's CCA became an outpost of Shetland for the day, no less than Aberdeen harbour does in the lead up to a sailing.

'Ken Wast Yell?' recalls a meeting of the Yell Film Club in the United Free Church in West Yell. In 'Carla's Song' Ken Loach explored the Nicaraguan conflict through a refugee in Glasgow, with Robert Carlyle playing the smitten bus driver who follows her back to Central America.

'Recline' is born of the great institution of the North boat, the film. Not only was it a good way for P&O to make even more money out of its passengers, it was the main form of entertainment for anyone too young to be served at the bar. They remain popular in the Northlink era for the same reasons.

This has been a rewarding process for me, and I'm really looking forward to seeing the rest of the work which has been produced.

The Corky
MARION FIONA MORRISON

The Corky
(*The Ardgowan Cinema in Glasgow*)

Early Saturday
We swarmed there, freshly scrubbed,
Brylcreem, Lifebuoy, Derbac soap.
Our jam jars
A ticket to heaven –
The smell of cork as incense.
The Pit – with its clattery wooden pews
Matins for the squalling hordes
Mesmerised to silence
By the roar of Metro Goldwyn Mayer.

We mastered America.
We swore allegiance to the flag
Held our intestines in at Pearl Harbour,
Spat insults with the best of the Chicago mobsters.
We counted those asdic pings in the North Atlantic
And when the reel guttered to a broken halt
We took to the stage in the Corky
And sang our party pieces
Blinking in the false light of real life
Until the pretend world ran again.
And as we lay dying with Jim Bowie,

The blood and the sweat in our eyes
We learned the cost of honour and freedom.

Back home, wrapped in our bedrolls at night
Our eyes rolled over the prairie
Of our fire-lit front room,
And we spun the barrels of our six guns,
Knowing we could conquer wild frontiers before
bedtime.

An Corcaidh

(Taigh-dhealbh Ardgowan ann an Glaschu)

Madainn Disathairne
Bha sinn mar sgaothaig chuileagan
Air ar sgùradh le Brylcreem, Lifebuoy, Siabann Derbac,
Grèim bàis air na crogain-silidh
Cead siubhail gu flaitheanas.
Fàileadh a' choirc' mar thùis
Am 'Pit' –
Na treastaichean maide le cladar
Aig 'matins' leis a' ghràisg
A-nis socair air sgàth
Na beucail aig MGM.

Bhuinnig sinn Ameireaga
Thug sinn bòidean dìlseachd don bhratach
Chùm sinn grèim air ar mionach aig Pearl Harbour
Thilg sinn sgalldaireachd mar eucoraich Chicago
Chùm sinn cunntas air na h-Asdic pings on Chuan Siar
Agus nuair a bhris an rìdhle le sglapadaich
Sheas sinn air an àrd-ùrlar as a' Chorcaidh
A' seinn àrd ar claiginn, a' dèanamh cèilidh
A' priobadh ar sùilean anns an t-solas mhealltach
Gus an do ruith an saoghal ìomhaigheach a-rithist
Gus an do laigh sinn sìos – a' bàsachadh le Jim Bowie
An fhuil agus am fallas nar sùilean

Ag ionnsachadh luach onair agus saorsa.

Aig an taigh a-rithist
Paisgte nar plaidaichean
Ri taobh ar teine
Ag amharc air prairies
An t-seòmair-shuidhe
A' cur charan air barailean ar piostalan
Cinnteach gun toir sin buaidh
Air Garbh Chrìochan Ameireaga
Mus tèid sinn a chadal a-nochd.

That Perfect Frame
AILSA THOM

I came to know them all: Greta Garbo. Katherine Hepburn. Clark Gable. Humphrey Bogart. All the beauties, and handsome men – my lovers, my brothers. I knew them intimately; that frown between their eyes when they were puzzled. The pitch of their voice when they were angry. How they made love, how they fought, how they died. I saw them change from energetically staccato images in black and white, to graceful fluid icons in colour: their faces, once smooth and fleshy, become lined and grave. But the curve of their lips, the luminosity of their eyes – these never changed.

I was 14 when my da told me I needn't go back to school on the Monday. The money I could earn was needed at home. Too young for the yards, he got me a job in the new cinema, the Grosvenor. The projectionist, Mr Lawson, looked an old man even then, although he must have only been in his forties, but shell-shock had left him gaunt and harried, and his hands trembled. The manager, Mr McIntosh, also bearing the scars of the Great War on his one good leg, had given him the job; two fellow survivors. Mr Lawson's trembling hands threatened to be his undoing, and they needed someone to do the fine work of threading the film through the projector. I was built like a Jack Russell my da said.

You needed to be strong to carry the cannisters of film, great metal cartwheels protecting the celluloid. But you needed to be small and nimble enough to squeeze into the space beside the projector to ease it back into life when it broke down, and your fingers precise enough to fit the perforations at the side of the film onto the feeder.

The Grosvenor was a handsome building of a vague Art Nouveau style, with one large screen seating 500 people in opulent surroundings. The organ was down the front, and Mrs Gardiner, who had lost her husband in the Boer War, and her three sons in the last war, played it with a tenderness which made grown men weep. Opening at 2pm and closing near midnight, six days a week, there was a constant showing of main features, B movies, short comedies, newsreels and documentaries. On Saturday mornings, children queued around the block, clutching jam jars and pennies in their chilblained fingers to watch the next exciting episode of the current serial, which, the week before, had left the hero literally hanging from a cliff. I envied them. Empty jam jars had been a rarity in my childhood, and I had seldom been allowed to join the queue.

I had imagined the job would be easy. You put the film on the projector, and the machinery runs it, right? But this was art. It was a ballet of precision and delicacy. You needed to be able to read the film, Mr Lawson said. Not just look out for that black dot in the top right-hand corner which meant it was almost time to change the reel, but listen to the clack and hiss of the film as it fed through the reels, sprockets and rollers, the sound changing incrementally as one rattling reel emptied and the other filled. The trick was with the timing, so that no one watching the film saw the gap. At first, I fumbled and blundered to get the reels changed in time. There would be boos and catcalls as the screen went white, their hero lurched away, reality rolled back at the audience with a suddenness which jarred.

Keeping the film feeding smoothly was another art. Sometimes the reel or the mechanism would stick and the celluloid would overheat, the image on the screen would melt and blacken. The smell in the small projection room was of death. Keeping the film moving was the way to protect it, but perversely also wore it out – lines, blotches and patchy tints infected the celluloid. Sometimes a hair would get inside the lens and wriggle and flicker across the screen. Once Myrna Loy wore a twitching hair-thin moustache as she fast-talk flirted with William Powell. Mr Lawson was furious. He loved Myrna.

The audience came in waves during the day. Ladies during the afternoon, clutching their shopping bags or their lovers. Men in greasy overcoats with nowhere else to go to keep out of the cold. Boys skiving school, and the girls come to find them. Bachelors delaying the inevitable return to empty digs came after work, followed by families, with courting couples being the last to leave. (All the stories you hear about the back row of the movies are true. But I never speak of them.) Clara was one of the usherettes. She wore the navy uniform with the red trim in a way which Gladys or Nancy never could, and she always gave a little wave towards the projection room, even though she couldn't see me. I had pretty much taken over from Mr Lawson by then. He would come in at 5pm, in time for the newsreel, and sit drinking tea from a thermos, topped up with something from a bottle he kept wrapped in brown paper in his overcoat pocket. He would have fallen asleep by the main feature, and wouldn't notice if I slipped in classic Laurel and Hardy now and again.

Mrs Gardiner had given up playing the organ, so we rarely showed the old silent films anymore. Sometimes, before the cinema opened for the day, I would play a reel of Clara Bow or Louise Brooks, just to watch their radiant skin and flashing eyes. These women didn't need to be heard – they spoke so clearly with just a look. By the end of the film, they might not always have won, but they had always changed the man in some devastating way.

My Clara devastated me in her own way. She married Mr McIntosh in a quiet ceremony one Saturday during the matinee. No one had thought that the bachelor with the tin leg would marry, let alone to a girl like Clara, but with the baby arriving just a few months later, he would have his hands full.

Another war came, and I was the perfect age to join up, the recruiting sergeant said. But, he added, it was a pity about my eye problem. But I didn't have any eye problem, I told him. He glared at me and told me to put my glasses back on and stop wasting his time. In vain I told him I didn't wear glasses. Mr Lawson grinned when I returned to the projection room that afternoon. "Projectionist's eye," he diagnosed, confidently.

My sight was perfect for seeing the actors on the screen at the far end of the auditorium. My sight was perfect for the close-up work on the projector and reading the film in negative. But I hadn't noticed that I was missing everything in-between. The optometrist told me that my lens bulged in 'an unusual way' and gave me glasses which, if I wore them, meant I couldn't see the screen or work the projector. That was a waste of 40 shillings.

Betty was the first woman to knock on the projection room door. She was in the WAAF and flew bombers from one airfield to another. Sometimes she came to the matinee and stayed on till we closed, then I wouldn't see her for days. That winter was icy fog and sleet, and Mr Lawson stayed at home in bed with a hacking cough. Betty kept me company, and for the first time in years, I was late in changing a reel. She laughed from the corner where she lay swathed in our coats as I scrambled, naked, to switch the reels, to the catcalls and jeers of both servicemen and civilians.

Then the bombs came, and the siren would empty the cinema. The shelters were dank and crowded, and a million miles away from the lives of debonair Cary Grant or sexy Veronica Lake. When the all-clear went, people didn't come back to the cinema – they wanted to get home to check that they still had a home to go to. Betty and I stayed in the projection room, and told each other we felt safe as we lay together in each other's arms. I would keep the film playing, just for her, sending the beam of light out through the smoky air like a beacon in the darkness. *Casablanca* was the soundtrack to my proposal.

Others began to stay, and slowly the audience grew until we had the reputation of never closing down, not even for Jerry. People reckoned we were just as safe in the warm and the dark with the flickering screen as we were in the shelters. When the all clear sounded, I would run the film backwards to the point where the bombs had begun to drown it out. Everyone applauded when I reached the right point, and I knew I was doing my bit for the war effort.

One night, Betty missed the landing lights in the fog and never came back. I showed comedy after comedy, all I could bear, ignoring Mr McIntosh's increasingly irate pleas to play the sentimental patriotic films he was contracted to.

After the war, people still somehow found the few coins to come to the pictures. There were, as after all wars, more women than men, but none came to my projection room. Mr Lawson had been lost in the rubble of his house, and Mr McIntosh took Clara and the children to live with his mother in Somerset. The new owner refurbished in chrome and plastic, and the organ was sold for scrap.

The films themselves changed, becoming more hopeful, more fantastic. No one wanted to see the reality of the bombsites and the damaged men and women. Actors grew even more handsome, the women more beautiful and sultry. Colour crept in, and blondes became all the rage, dizzying in their bright dresses and scarlet lips. Most of the movies came from America, where the people looked sleek and elegant; another species entirely.

The projector was updated: the massive machinery broken up and replaced with something smaller in metals and plastic. They needed space to store the swathe of new movies, and I was asked to catalogue the old celluloid cannisters, the silents to be sent for destruction. I found that I could carry four reels at a time under my coat, with two in my satchel. I emptied the lawnmower out of the shed, and began to stack them up. But this wasn't enough, and one day I returned to the cinema to find that nothing before 1930 existed anymore. Everyone was looking forward: no one wanted to look back.

Television tried to steal my audience, but quiz shows and music programmes could never fully compete. Marylin Munro, Ava Gardner, Jane Russell – you needed to see them three times their size to fully appreciate their magic. Musicals continued to be popular, and gangster movies, but cowboys and child-star films seemed to dip and disappear.

Then something strange happened, and the films became both modern and nostalgic at the same time. They showed the world as it currently was, but still told the old stories I recognised, only the faces were new.

The Grosvenor was bought over by a chain, and there was talk of closing it and making it into a shop which sold only frozen food, but nothing came of that.

The projector got smaller again, and all the cannisters were all finally removed, new films simply borrowed from a supplier on a week-to-week basis. I was showing fewer and fewer shorts or B movies, and the news and documentaries had dried up, fodder for the television.

This new management suggested that I might like a retirement package, but what was I to retire to? A shed full of silent movies which I couldn't watch, an empty house with a lawnmower in the spare room. I worked on, and suffered the string of spotty youths who came to do work experience, as it was called. Mainly they smoked and looked bored – arcade games their real calling.

Video machines nearly killed us off, but then there were few new movies worthy of being seen on the big screen anyway. I didn't recognise any of the faces any-more – even the familiar names were too altered by time.

Then the Grosvenor was finally sold off, and became a bingo hall. I scoured the storerooms, persuaded one of the spotty youths to search the attic, and managed to take home some more films which had been overlooked. Sometimes, I would take one from its cannister and hold it up to the light, watching the film in the slowest of motion as I pulled it through my fingers.

My life dragged in slow motion too until a young woman from a newspaper phoned and asked to visit me. She looked a little bit like Betty, and had something of Betty's boldness in her eyes, so I found that I spoke to her more than I had spoken to anyone in a long time. She agreed that my shed full of films couldn't possibly be counted as theft, and called me a champion of the movies. The house seemed empty without her, and I contemplated getting the bus to the nearest cinema, but it was out of town and the bus didn't go that far.

I donated the contents of my shed to a new museum of cinema, and was hailed a hero for my foresight in 'preserving' them. I tried to give them the lawnmower too. Something else I had no more use for.

A few months later, the phone rang again; a curiously empty sound. There was to be a gala reopening of an independent cinema in the town centre – a competitor in the old days, which had once tried to poach me. I found myself guest of honour, and told some of my little stories about my days as a projectionist to the audience, before we watched a full show of a newsreel, B movie and main feature. There was no projectionist now – an employee in a T-shirt just pressed a button on a box and went to have ice cream, and a digital recording sent the image to the screen.

The films had been 'cleaned up' they said, no lines or jumps or marks. No errant hairs. I missed that. The films no longer had a life of their own – no one would ever be able to make the images slow down or speed up. No longer could the movie be stopped, and sent running backwards to the chosen point in the past. To that perfect frame, where I could have saved more than just the film.

Spencer Tracy and the Peerie Boy
DAVID SINCLAIR
& RICHARD CLUBLEY

The tiny Orkney island of Flotta has a population of about 60 today. During my childhood there were probably around 200 folk living here, but by 1943 we had a state-of-the-art cinema big enough to seat 1200 in considerable comfort. The whole island community could sit together in the balcony. I was born here, on 27th April 1935. My name is David Sinclair, I am 83 years old.

When war came to Flotta in 1939 the school roll was boosted by children of service men and women based on the island. There were about 40 of us in the school so we were never short of pals, or mischief to get into. Scapa Flow, the huge, natural harbour enclosed by the islands of Orkney, became the base for the Home Fleet, as it had been during World War One. At the peak of hostilities there were 40,000 army, navy and air force personnel in Orkney, all associated with the comings and goings of the fleet and swelling the population to about three times its peace-time number. There were sailors, of course, plus anti-aircraft crews on shore, radar, searchlight, barrage balloon operators, catering and supply people and medics. There was everything needed to keep this huge fighting force supplied, equipped, defended – and entertained.

A posting to Orkney was not always popular. Some folk enjoyed it if they had a comfortable billet and could get to the town for the regular dances and so forth. If you were assigned to a searchlight or a gun on a bleak, windswept hillside or shore, however, then life might not be so comfortable. Orkney winters are tough. 'Bloody Orkney' someone called it. The wind can be unrelenting.

Mindful of the need to maintain morale the naval authorities at Lyness on the island of Hoy, and on Flotta close-by, built a considerable entertainment complex to which soldiers and sailors could repair for what would be called R&R today. On Flotta there were squash courts, a gymnasium, dance hall, and two NAAFI and also several army camps with canteens that sold beer, while non-alcoholic beverages were available in the two Church of Scotland huts.

They also provided a brick-built cinema, to replace the old wooden one. It seated 1236, including 200 in the grand, raked balcony. It had a fitted stage for live drama and music performances and, when opened in July 1943 by Admiral Sir Bruce Fraser, it had state-of-the-art theatre lighting. Arthur Askey and Jack Hylton both performed at the opening event. Later, Gracie Fields, Yehudi Menuhin and George Formby came to entertain the troops. Someone told me recently that her mum had worked in the NAAFI at Flotta and remembers George

Formby having to run off after each number and swap his ukulele for a re-tuned one, such were the fluctuating atmospheric conditions. Tommy Handley's popular radio show "It's That Man Again" was recorded here.

The cinema was always packed, mostly with ships' companies that had been given leave to jump on a liberty boat, a sort of water taxi, and come ashore for the afternoon or evening. With so many warships at anchor they had to take turns. There was never any shortage of enthusiastic audiences.

I was eight years old when the cinema opened and well remember the excitement of watching films there. We had no television, only the most basic of radio sets. I recall being smuggled in to some screenings by the men who often took pity on us island children. Whether the 'smuggling' was to avoid payment I cannot bring to mind. I do remember watching *The Seventh Cross* with Spencer Tracy. It frightened me and I watched through my fingers mostly.

The cinema was a magnificent, sturdy, brick construction. Three walls, including the foyer and projection room, are still standing in 2018, although the latter has a tree growing through the top. The auditorium roof of corrugated asbestos sheets was sold to a Kirkwall garage years ago. The end wall, supporting the screen, was knocked down to provide a storage space for building materials during the construction of the Flotta

Oil Terminal in 1974.

The Naval Cinema on Flotta was built to last. They had no idea, in 1943, how much longer the war was going to drag on, or how long after that Scapa Flow would be needed as a fleet base. In the event it was boarded up sometime in the 1950s, never to be used again. In our later childhood we had further adventures climbing in through vents, windows or any way we could find. Each time we broke in the authorities boarded up the hole but we always found another. Some involved climbing drain pipes. In this way the cinema continued to provide excitement and adventure, long after Spencer Tracy had left.

I suppose the very best cinema experiences have us on the edge of our seats, one way or another. Passion, comedy, suspense, intrigue, adventure and fear can all do this. Spencer Tracy certainly frightened me. I had stood with my family as bombs dropped near our quiet, rural, island home so was no stranger to fear. The movies, though, can seem just as real. After the Naval Cinema closed life would never be quite the same again. Windows onto too many other worlds had been opened. For a time all that was left was climbing into the lifeless shell in search of adventure – and, maybe, a little bit of the fear we had lost.

Note: Peerie is an Orkney dialect word meaning 'small'.

Peerie is often replaced by Peedie today but this writer clings staunchly to the old words. In 1943, when this story is set, it would most certainly have been peerie.

Here Come the Movies
SYLVIA ANNE TELFER

SCRIPT: 'HERE COME THE MOVIES'

O.S.
A BLUE MAN OF THE MINCH crawls onto shore
shaken to the core over the blotch of blue,
a seized kin, he's spotted on ferry.

FLASHBACK to 'I Know Where I'm Going' in which
a bride-to-be's cut off by blue men squalls,
falls in love with local laird instead, then

FAST-FORWARD to 'S.S. Politician'
in 'Whisky Galore', another casualty
of blue men's Force Ten intention.

ESTABLISHING SHOT:
Blue Screen Machine truck aka blue man's kin
rolls onto Barra, a snake shedding skin,
for the showing "the morra",
when islanders will teleport to India.

ACTION
Driver-projectionist IAIN MACCOLL's the soul
of the truck, and to locals' gasp
fairy-godmother-swells it into cinema
while blue man recalls 'Katrina'.

INT.
A local plonked in plush red seat grows
fidgety for 'Slumdog Millionaire'
while raucous teenagers bag the back rows.
Usher crochets. Lights dim.

O.S.
Ghost of the first Barra Viking,
'Omund the wooden-leg',
lands in his long ship, stumps up
the wheelchair access. No-one notices
him or the 'not now got a foggy' blue man.

ACTION
MacColl shines TORCH from projection
box to shoo an astray fox, unlocks
a 35mm film. Reels on wheels begin to spin.

      MACCOLL (muttering to himself)
      Better if we never see digital.

FADE OUT

O.S.
MacColl heads for Tobermory,
Isle of Arran and Loch Carron
while just-seen-a-blue moon blue man,
who now doesn't give a hoot about ocean,
sets off in spaceraft in hot pursuit.

70

3

UNFORGETTABLE PEOPLE

The Highlands and Islands Film Guild: A Touch of the Exotic: Shetland memories from the mid-1950s
CHRISTINE DE LUCA

I have vivid memories of the Highlands and Islands Film Guild van coming to Waas, the village on the west side of mainland Shetland where I was brought up. Among the school children, anticipation was palpable. The notice had been printed in the previous Friday's *Shetland Times*. We'd waited … was it a whole month? Tonight would be magical!

Waas (meaning 'inlets of the sea') was well named. Houses nestled snugly round the voe (the inlet) and, beyond that, the crofting–fishing township sprawled: Brig o Waas to the east and, to the west, Mid-Waas and Dale o Waas. Little groupings of crofts, all with descriptive Norse names, spread across the western extremities of the island: Brunnatwatt, Vesquoy, Skeotaing, Trölligart. The Film Guild van would leave the tarred single-track road as it came near the village and approach the hall with a *styooch* of gravel under the tyres. Few people had cars in those days and many who came to the films would have walked a fair distance. In the remoter hamlets the shop van was indispensable. One hardy old crofter still rowed across the voe for his messages. Even fewer people had a telephone. And no one had electricity. Several households had large wooden wireless sets with acid batteries which had to be re-charged and huge valves which were apt to blow. Television was many years away. Films were something other people saw.

Within the family circle, the wireless was a source of entertainment as well as news. With no central heating, whole families tended to spend a lot of time together in the living room where there was a stove and lamps. I can still remember at my maternal grandmother's house in Cunningsburgh, how a cousin walked across the valley daily to spend half an hour with his relatives, listening to the news on the wireless.

Comics were still a bit of a luxury as were illustrated books. The nearest cinema (*The North Star*) was 25 miles or more away and beyond the pocket of most families. And the bus service didn't run in the evening. Visually it was all inside our heads or out there in the real world. There was plenty community-based, home-made entertainment but what the Film Guild brought us was an entirely new world; an exciting otherness quite different from our daily experience. No wonder there was anticipation.

Our projectionist-operator was George Horne, a tall, Scalloway man. To us he was our Gregory Peck: on the cusp of 'dashing' with his trim moustache; straight out of a film. While he was quiet and unflappable, he was also friendly. And he was, above all, technically competent and dependable. He travelled all over the mainland to the smaller rural communities. He would arrive in the Commer van (was it black with white lettering on the side, or white with black lettering?), park it near the door of the village hall, run the cables into the hall from the petrol generator in the back of the van, and set up the 16mm projector and screen. The caretaker would have set out all the wooden forms in advance, ranked down each side of the hall. The curtains were closed and the paraffin heater lit. It would be many years before the forms were replaced with chairs. So there were no 'better' seats to be had. As children, the premium was on a front seat. Someone must have been delegated to collect the money as we flocked in. It was perhaps threepence for a child. The sudden whirr of the projector, the strong beam of light, the sound and then the pictures! It was totally absorbing. Silence fell.

My strongest memory seems to be of wild-west, cowboy films. I had a pair of shorts with cowboys on the pockets which I loved wearing. I liked cap guns and cowboy hats. This was right up my street. My sister Joy remembers the *Marx Brothers* and being very scared by their antics! Similarly, my friend Iris remembers *The Green Man*, a comedy which rather terrified her as a little girl when, on lifting the lid of a grand piano, a dead body appeared!

Usually there would be something suitable for

children at the start (perhaps a cartoon or a 'wholesome' short film) and *Pathe News*. Usually we were expected home after that but we would plead to stay on and see the feature film, like the grown-ups. Sometimes we were allowed to, if the film was deemed suitable. *White Christmas* was a memorable one, sitting in the front row with our mother.

There was no interval that I remember – no cups of tea and certainly no ice cream or popcorn. Just a natural break when reels had to be changed as quickly as possible and off we'd go again.

The day would come when we'd be able to drive the 25 miles to *The North Star* to see the film about the coronation, *A Queen is Crowned.* My only other cinema experience pre-age 15 was the comedy *Cheaper by the Dozen,* a film about a large family. So what the Highlands and Islands Film Guild brought us was a unique combination of novelty and interest; education, entertainment and a touch of the exotic! Happy days!

Shoot oot at da Waas Public Hall
CHRISTINE DE LUCA

In memoriam George Horne, Projectionist,
Highlands & Islands Film Guild (1946-1971)

Da hall wis sweepit, benches set
for da Highlands an Islands man
at cam wi da montly films. Dey wir
da peerie pictir for wis bairns, sae,
tripenny-bits i wir löfs, we widged
wirsels on ta widden forms, tinkin
twa-bob couldna buy a better ticket.

Oh, we'd seen pictirs afore, trowe viewers
held ta wir een, an a lever ta push doon,
scene eftir scene. But dis wis da rael thing.
Twa muckle wheels a-whirr, stoor catcht
i da beam, da scratcht black flitterin stert,

da sudden soondtrack, da dazzlin pictirs.
We wir stumsed, hüld i da spell.

Half time, an da reel wis changed;
catcht quick afore, clickity-click,
hit birled aff an spooled owre da flör.
Hit wis magic; an whin da cowboys hung
affa der horses, shastin da stagecoach,
an a boy tummelled fae his saet,
we could a swörn he'd been shot.

Electric Palaces
RUTH HOWELL

Cinema was in my father's blood. Aged two, his consciousness awoke in the front row of the Capitol Cinema, Belfast. A twenty-foot-high Roy Rogers was playing a guitar and singing a nice song to his horse, Trigger. Dad was alone in the thousand-seater auditorium, clad only in a nappy. He was not afraid; in one way or another, he'd already spent most of his life in the cinema. The air was warm and fuggy, loaded with the comforting aromas of nicotine and horsehair, although the red plush seat was slightly scratchy on his bare legs. On the floor in front of him, beside The Mighty Wurlitzer Cinema Organ, a pile of jam jars glowed in rainbow colours, illuminated by the slab of light from the projector room high in the back wall. All of these things, along with The Singing Cowboy and His Four-Legged Friend – a horse so clever that he could untie ropes and shoot a gun – combined to create a moment of beauty and clarity and perfection that stayed with him till the end of his life.

Great Grandpa was born near Belfast in 1872. He had nine younger siblings. Like many poor boys of the day, he left school at an early age, barely able to read and write. By the age of twelve he was working on the roads. He was hungry, tough, curious. While he dug ditches and barrowed stone, his dreams were full of sparks. Electricity was then a dangerous new phenomenon, a parlour trick for the rich and fashionable. He sensed that it might be captured, harnessed and enslaved, like a genie in a bottle. There was much more than magic in it. As he set about discovering the secrets of electric light illumination, the Lumière brothers were perfecting the first motion picture film camera.

Great Grandpa learned fast. He worked, he travelled, he noticed the gaps where a smart lad might squeeze himself through to a brighter, more colourful world. Before long he had set himself up as an electrical engineer. By the end of the First World War he had bought the wreckage of two German U-boats for a knock-down price, stripping out the great diesel engines and using them to build a power station. He dreamed of light, of electrified palaces. So he built cinemas. He began with six, one for each of his sons. Grandpa was given the Capitol. He did not get to choose.

In 1941 my Dad stood with his siblings on the Cave Hill above Belfast and watched as the bombs rained down. The whole city seemed to be on fire. Somewhere in the middle of it were the palaces his grandfather had built.

In 1968 my Dad took me to Dublin for a shopping trip. As a special treat he said he would take me to see a film. I was glad to get out of Belfast for a few days;

aged six, I was dimly aware that things were turning ugly in my home town. Some delicate balance had been disturbed, and the world I thought I knew was running out of focus.

Until that point, cinema had meant Disney. It had meant *The Aristocats*, *Sleeping Beauty*, *Cinderella*. It had meant luminous colour and animation, talking broomsticks and silly songs. But this cinema, and this film, were very different.

The Dublin cinema was unlike any I'd seen before. I remember a vast dome, like a planetarium, and individual white plastic seats with tangerine and lime green cushions. Everything else was black. As the lights went down, I was transported. On the giant screen a wheel waltzed gracefully in space. A woman carrying a tray walked calmly up a wall. A red-eyed computer menaced an astronaut, who turned into a baby. I didn't understand any of it. What I did understand was that the dome with the tangerine and lime green cushions and the wheel in space were part of the same future, the same vision. Everything did not have to fall apart. I had discovered what my Dad already knew; cinema was a place of refuge.

Over the next twenty years, cinema was the portal to another place, a better place, for my siblings and me. Around us, lives were ending without meaning. Our town had two traditions, two narratives, two formats, which were incompatible. They had been inexpertly spliced together and, day by day, the fragile join was failing. Our days were full of stories that were not good stories, well told.

But even in the worst times, we dared the streets for the cinema, where the narratives still made sense. We queued up in the centre of town, beside the bombed-out remains of the Europa Hotel where, high above our heads, the purple curtains flapped raggedly in the rain. We waited avidly for every new release, craving the magic moments when the lights dimmed and the jaunty Pearl and Dean theme blasted out from the Dolby Sound speakers. When the British Board of Film Classification certificate appeared on the screen, all was still right with the world. And every film, good or bad, was greeted with the same breathless hush. Even the wail of sirens or the crump of a distant blast could not transport us back to the real world. We stayed quiet in the darkness and held on tight to better versions of ourselves.

When the Capitol was destroyed, Dad and I went to see it one last time. He didn't say a word as the palace his grandfather built was bulldozed into the ground. I held my breath as the front wall collapsed and the entrails of the air-conditioning system were suddenly exposed, flopping out of the roof space like the intestines of some giant animal. The metal cans in the film store slithered off their stacks and burst open, showering the street with spirals the colour of dried blood. I remembered every film I'd seen there. I remembered them because they'd become part of me.

Today, despite the many other options available to him, my son prefers to see films in the cinema. He doesn't really know why. But something flickers in his veins: twenty-four frames a second, spooling through his cells, recording his memories and experiences in some intangible segment of his DNA. I hope some day he'll discover for himself what I already know.

Cinema is in his blood.

The Projectionist
GEORGINA COBURN

There's comfort in darkness, like being held in the womb waiting to be born. Embraced by the wonder of creation, shielded in the crimson glow of cushioned upholstery, I become open to the world and all its possibilities in ways I never could be outside. Like the hands of a lover, covering your eyes for guess who, transforming the sun into the pure warmth of skin and peach stained luminescence, I know this place by touch. You could blindfold me, and I would still find the way to my seat in this cavernous underworld, sinking into the relief of anonymity, melting into the silent audience unseen. Untold horrors may loom large on screen and beyond these walls, but here I have always felt safe.

My father is memory and ash cast far out to sea, but he's always here, sitting behind me in the dark, tending a fire that never goes out. Flickering in the enchanted half-light, his lighthouse beam of imagination guides me away from the rocks, suspended in light, hope and particles of human dust. He's there in a black box compartment of my mind, charming and ageless with his matinee idol looks, splicing the story I tell myself together, editing my memories. I think of him as the soothing hum of flickering time, held within each frame and breath, defying absence and celluloid decay. My chemical inheritance is flame-burst volatile silver nitrate and the threat of self-immolation. But it is also the pure truth of fiction, illuminated in all the lives, memories and experiences that ever were or will be projected on screen. All our fears and desires, held inside each silhouette, in every row and generation, wave upon wave. My father is a keeper of dreams, holding the movement of ages gently between his fingertips, holding the film up to the light, looking for flaws to be mended, restoring worlds.

In the magic of the darkroom, the lone projectionist's booth and the lush cave of the auditorium, I learned that everything I need is here, everything I dream, am nourished by and aspire to. Like a deep-sea diver hooked up to pure oxygen, the discoveries are endless, reflected in the sparkling blue delight of my father's eyes. I can hold my shark-circling fears at arm's length until the film, like air, runs out. Down here there are creatures so strange, without name or classification, cast adrift into dark matter. Held in the eye and growing into the most delicate of organisms many fathoms deep, my precious embryo imaginings are aglow and pulsing with life. I drink all that I see until I drown. Drifting in the languid current, softly undulating forests of seaweed, bleached silence and darting fish eyes attend my dreams. Awakened and surfacing, reborn in shock and disbelief, I gasp like a fish suffocating on air, gulping sorrow and sharp regret. It catches in my throat, like the barbed thought that I cannot remain beneath the waves, cloaked in emerald and ultramarine, your silver darling.

With you the fun and tears never stopped, you lived life with the breathless pace of an action blockbuster, never dull, but lacking something you never chose to be. Now when I try to remember your face it is a rush of feeling, a hard, rough slap like the wave you told me never to turn my back on, teaching me how to swim to outwit the undertow. Entangled in spools of kelp and all the stills you ever shot, I was never too young to learn. I lived in the Black and White Romance of your movie books, the crafted tableaux of the studio and your symphonic record collection. I remember your riotous slapstick humour and abdication of responsibility mum never shared, the home movie of you swinging on a rope in an animal skin as Tarzan, spoofing the MGM lion roaring in the credits. The thought of your perfectly lip-synced king of the studio jungle still makes me smile. Your dress-ups were genius, Roman Centurion nobility and goofy Herman Munster. You could construct anything. You carved me masks in Primary School that I've worn all my life. I live always for another moment of bliss, atonement and wonder, like the monochrome world turning Technicolor in my childhood land of Oz. All those hot summers ago, just the three of us at the drive-in, van doors flung open to a nightscape of chirruping insects, eating ice-cream under the stars in front of a screen bigger than Jupiter, more luminous and fantastical than Méliès's smiling moon.

Here in the North your fierce light is refracted in blue remembrance, held below the equator in another hemisphere, beneath the warm winter waves of the Indian Ocean when it rains. My world is turned to ice and as my breath quickens it crystalises into white vapour, diminishing into a phantom of distant light. I find myself living through visions and I look for you everywhere, in people, peals of laughter and the eternal, pristine beauty of monochrome. Sitting next to you I hold my own hand, submerged in your half-lit smile, an ocean of inaudible sound between us. In time there will be no ships or oceans to carry me away, split into a myriad of atoms and scattered sunlight, waiting to begin. Soon opaque silver-gelatin cataracts will cover my eyes, my greatest loss not being able to see, or even know, who you really were.

Here's Looking at You, Kid
DONALD MCKENZIE

'Dae ah huv tae go.'

'Aye, ye kin keep me company when yer mither's at her training.'

Fingal McErc was not best pleased. His mother had announced a few weeks earlier that she was taking up chiropody as a part-time occupation after she and his father would retire. His mother had been left a small cottage and croft in the Outer Hebrides. Fingal just couldn't get his head around the surreal nature of the situation.

'Cutting auld folks' toenails on Benbecula. Ah mean – they aw wear wellingtons. Whit kind o' state are their feet gaun tae be in? Whau in thur right mind wid want tae be daein that?'

'Whit wis that ye said?' asked his mother.

'Nuthin,' he muttered.

Reluctantly he followed them out to the car for the hour-long journey. It was 1968 and as a 17-year-old all he wanted to do was listen to Velvet Underground tracks and not be spending the longest and most boring afternoon of his life listening to his father pontificating on this, that and the other between renditions of Perry Como ballads. He felt borderline suicidal. Even the weather reflected his mood. It was raining heavily, and

87

as they drove past the grey tenements on the outskirts of the city he thought they could have just as easily been driving through a wintry Siberian Vladi-bloody-vostok as Glasgow; it looked that miserable. He glanced at the tied canvas roll on the seat beside him that contained his mother's scalpels, snips and files; a roll that also held other instruments of the Devil that were apparently essential to pare, excise and scrape away any condition from a verruca to a corn. His father had said when he first saw this set of gleaming tools that his mother would know her onions from her bunions in no time at all.

Fingal wondered if she was a KGB torturer on her way to question some double agent that was being held prisoner in a 'safe house' in Rutherglen but he also suspected that at some point in the weeks, perhaps months, to come she would be looking for victims to practise on. He knew this was a woman who took great delight in squeezing the pimples and blackheads on his nose and forehead, one who would use the curved end of a hair grip to clean out the wax from his ears, and to her a big yellow red-tipped pustule on the back of his neck was a thing of beauty and a ripening challenge to look forward to. She was ambitious if nothing else and chiropody apparently was something to aspire to.

'Ah must huv been adopted,' he thought. 'These people cannae be ma parents.'

The car crunched over the gravel drive leading to

88

a rather imposing looking house. His father kept the engine running as his mother made her way to the door and rang the bell. As the door opened, a few words were spoken, and she turned and nodded to his father. Fingal started to climb into the vacated front seat.

'*Wu've goat aw efternoon – wid ye like tae go tae a tea dance son?*'

Fingal froze, went pale and felt sick.

'*Crivens. This cannae be happening tae me,*' he was thinking.

'*Jist joking. Let's go tae the cinema.*'

'*Aye – that wid be guid,*' he said with obvious relief as the roar of panic in his ears subsided and his heartbeat started to return to normal. His father laughed.

'*Aye – it's been some time since ah wis at the cinema. Used to be that two jeelly jars wid get ye in.*'

'*Aye, right,*' said Fingal.

'*Naw. Ah'm telling ye. It's true. Anyway, disnae matter. I hear there's one o' these Cinerama picture hooses nearby. Converted the Coliseum so they did, an it's the first wan in Scotland ah believe. Thur showing Whaur Eagles Dare.*'

His father was obviously in poseur mode as he joked with the woman in the ticket booth – repeating the jam-jar story. Fingal wasn't sure who he was showing off to but suspected it was him and all he felt was deep embarrassment. Listening to his father effectively trying to chat-up a cinema ticket seller was beyond the pale.

'*Aye, ah've no heard that wan afore like,*' she said – the face unmoving and as stony as an Easter Island statue. There was a short silence.

'*Well, one an' a half fur the front circle then hen.*'

'*Ah think that'll be twa adults,*' she said looking at Fingal.

'*Oh, aye, awright.*'

'*Five shillings,*' she said. Fingal's father's face turned grey and there was a definite tremble in his hands as he counted out the coins. Fingal thought his father was about to faint. Things were looking up – this was more like it. This would be killing him.

Fingal had never been inside such a large cinema. They took two seats in the middle of the front row of the lower circle. The auditorium was almost empty. It seemed not a lot happened on a Tuesday or perhaps the cost of entry was a deterrent to people accustomed to paying less to see a movie. The curtains swished open to reveal the massive curved screen and Fingal was astonished. As the opening scene rolled his heart thumped to the drumbeat of the overture. His field of vision filled with an aerial view of snow-clad mountains. His eyes were as saucers but even so, he couldn't see the edges of the screen and he believed he was truly flying. Fingal's heart soared joyously with the build-up of the music but then he instinctively ducked when a plane seemed to hurtle out of the screen towards him. He laughed nervously at his reaction but was transfixed. He was in that plane, believed he was sitting beside the soldiers, and was ready to parachute out. Here was a new reality and he was part of it.

Fingal was silent in the car as they drove home. His mother was also tight-lipped after his father made some comment when he saw a man hobbling down the street a short distance from the mansion – asking how many toes he had left. She never returned to the course, but the implements of torture were taken to the Hebrides. Years later in moments of quiet reflection Fingal could still recall times when he would visit them in their retirement and the sound of goats bleating forlornly in the shed could be heard as his mother attended to their hooves.

Four years later Fingal found himself back in Glasgow. No longer a boily boy but a young man excited to be starting his first job. His parents were so pleased that they had bought him a new leather coat from an outfitter in Ingram Street; too big for him by at least one size as for some reason his mother thought he would grow into it. Fingal had studiously avoided work by staying on at school for as long as possible and then to college. All to no avail as University was all too sadly out of the reach of his mental capabilities. *Que Sera Sera* as his father used to sing, (he was also fond of Doris Day), but his parents were very relieved to see him 'settled.' He had secured work in an Employment Exchange. A Civil Servant no less.

'A joab fur life son,' his proud father ominously predicted.

The office was located on a lozenge-shaped piece of land beside the local cemetery. He learned that it had once been the location for a cinema nicknamed locally as 'The Coffin' due to its shape and proximity to the graveyard. About a month after he had started work he was sitting in the staff tearoom looking at the view from the window. This window had bars and wire netting to protect the building from the local Comancheros. He thought it was not so much an office – more like Fort Apache. There were several imposing sepulchres in the boneyard that reminded him of the Roman tombs along the Appian Way. He had seen them during a school trip and recalled also being in the Forum to be shown the spot where Brutus had plunged his dagger into Caesar. His teenage outing with his father had been the beginning of a love of the cinema. Motion pictures were his means of escape from the reality of life. Fingal thought of Charlton Heston playing Brutus; imagining his line manager as Caesar. If only he had decided to become an actor and not a Civil Servant, his life could have been so different. He turned just as the staffroom door opened and he saw the most beautiful girl he had ever seen. Forget Monroe, forget Taylor, forget Hayworth, forget them all. Reality had just overwhelmed make-believe. Fingal was stunned into a jaw-dropping wide-eyed paralysis. The new girl swished past him in an outfit that buttoned up the front from hem to neckline. He groaned like Major Danby in Catch 22.

It took a week for Fingal to garner enough courage to ask her for a date. He had discovered her name was Eilidh and was now aware that when she did see him in the tearoom she tended to blush. All was meticulously planned. His attraction was such that all fear of rejection was suppressed although he reckoned she was so good-looking he didn't stand a chance. He would wait until one of the busiest days of the week, a Thursday or Friday when all the local unemployed men came in to 'sign on' and receive payment. He would be a cashier and he knew Eilidh would be on duty to clear any payment queries that arose. His chance came.

'*Query. Query,*' he shouted and she came to his side. Fingal gave her the coupon with the payment details that were at odds with the register and whispered, '*Wid ye like tae go oot wi me?*'

'*I don't think so,*' she said in a very loud voice.

Fingal was mortified. It was as if he had been slapped and could feel the burn on his face. His chest tightened and his mind was befuddled. Everyone was looking at him and laughing and that included the clients.

'*Cheeky bugger,*' he thought. '*Ah'll no be asking her oot again.*'

'*Get a move oan pal. Ah've goat a taxi waitin ootside,*' said the next man in the queue. It was a very long morning.

Fingal was sitting at his desk later that day when the phone rang. It was Eilidh.

'*Yes, I would like to go out with you. I just didn't want the others to know.*'

Fingal almost wept.

It was raining and Fingal was in a rush. He wasn't sure how he had managed to leave things so late but he had. He was to meet Eilidh for their date underneath the 'dissy' clock on the Boots Building in Argyle Street and intended taking her to the cinema. '*The Godfather, she'll like that okay,*' he assumed, seeing as it had just been released. The 'dissy' thing had confused him when someone in the office mentioned it. He was told this was Glasgow slang for being 'stood up' as any girl would not linger there if her date was not on time. He was wearing the new leather coat, thinking this would impress her. The rain was streaming off the bottom edge and had soaked the front of his trousers. He shuddered to think how that was going to look. As he hurtled across the wet cobbles towards the local underground station he suddenly slipped, sailed headlong through the air and landed face down in a puddle. He lay winded and stunned. In front of him he saw a crushed pink cigarette packet floating down the gutter; Passing Clouds. How prophetic he thought.

His problem about appearing incontinent had been resolved as from waist to toe it now appeared that he had waded across the River Kelvin. There was pain in his hand with blood oozing from grazed skin; blood that looked horribly black in the acidic flickering light coming from a nearby streetlamp. He thought of Wilde and looked up to the heavens but there wasn't a star in sight; just inky blackness. He heard the rustle of leaves, the rain was slanting through the orange glow from the lamp and he was aware of a waft of warmth coming from the entrance to the station. It was as if time had stopped.

'*Crivens, ah better get a move oan,*' he muttered with renewed determination. '*Ah'm no' giving up that easily.*'

He staggered to his feet. His coat was scuffed and now looked as if it had been bought from a charity shop. He stumbled into the foyer, explained his situation to the ticket booth attendant and asked if there was a place where he could wash his hands and try to tidy himself up a bit.

'*Ah cannae let ye in son,*' said the woman in the booth. '*Security n'that.*'

Fingal looked at her and asked, *'Did ye ever work in the Cinerama? Ye look kinda familiar.'*

'Naw son,' she said. *'Mibbae ye're thinking o' the La Scala.'*

Fingal paid for his ticket and headed towards the stairs for the platform.

'Haud oan son.'

Fingal turned. The woman was pushing a wet rag through the glass slot of the booth.

'Another minute and I would have left,' he was informed when he met Eilidh – but he had made it. If nothing else it was worth it just to see the look on the faces of the other males standing about when she took his hand and he knew that they couldn't comprehend why he was Mr Lucky – but then again, he couldn't quite believe it himself.

Forty-five years later Fingal was in his cottage in Benbecula. Eilidh's death was something he was still in denial about. It had been two years now. Looking back, he thought of his life and what kind of movie might have been made about it; romance, comedy, thriller, tragedy … Probably all these things. He picked up a hair grip, closed his eyes with pleasure as he poked it in his ear and on removal studied the wax as if he was admiring a masterpiece in a gallery. He wiped it on his jersey and put it back in his pocket. *'Everything dies and stays dead,'* he thought. On the table before him he had opened the roll of chiropody tools. He selected the largest scalpel, looked at the spots of rust on the blade, and considered the possibilities.

'No much point tae anything really. Jist the passing of the days noo,' he thought.

There was a crash of gears as the Screen Machine passed the house on its way to the local hotel car-park to set up for that night's film show.

Fingal sighed, put the scalpel back in its place and re-tied the roll.

Hogmanay
KAY RITCHIE

Maybe she was scrubbing, polishing away the old,
having dressed him in his Sunday best
sent him to swap jam-jars for tuppence at Galbraith's –
his entrance fee to the matinee
that final day.

Maybe he found a seat or had to stand amidst
the brothers and sisters and babies and friends
and cowboys on the silent screen.
Maybe when the woman played the upright
he sang-along

Are you comin to the Glen?
Are you comin wi' me?

Maybe when they shouted out *FIRE*
he joined the stampede,
leapt from the balcony, fell down stairs,
choked from the reek of
nitrate, vomit.

Or maybe he was already barefoot, limbs
tangled like unwound celluloid
spooling under layers of bodies
caught around another's legs
like wayward shoelace.

Unaware.

*(In memorium of Harry Green, aged 5, one of the 71
children killed from asphyxia and crushing at the Glen
Cinema, Paisley, December 31st, 1929. His small clogs
are displayed in Paisley Museum.)*

4

MEMORABLE FILMS

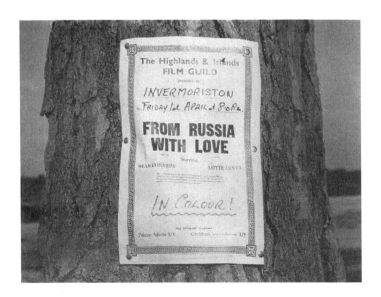

The Last Reel
ALISON MILLER

That was her first mistake, turning up to Assembly to show face, when she knew fine she'd be skinning school before the day was done.

Harry, oh Harry!

Sando caught her in the corridor on the way to French with Isabel.

'Eva, I'd like a word with you today after your last class. Come and see me in my office.'

What could she say?

'Yes, sir.'

Yes, sir! When she had no intention whatsoever of missing her time with Harry. How could she? Issy rolled her eyes in sympathy, which made her look slightly mad. Her eyebrows were plucked so high since she met Huw, she looked permanently surprised, even when she wasn't pulling a face.

'What way does Sando never pick on you, Issy? You skin school just as much. You're at the flicks with Huw every other day.'

'Oh,' she said, 'my natural charm, I suppose.' And she pulled the pleats of her school skirt tight round her hips and wiggled her bum in the gloom of the corridor. 'The Betty Grable of the north, that's me.'

'Ha, ha! I don't imagine Betty Grable goes about in

shoes clarted with gutter!'

It was after two before Eva escaped and ran down the Strynd to the Albert Kinema. Nobody was about in School Place till an army truck passed with a bunch of squaddies in the back and a few of them whistled and shouted DARLIN! at her. The day was still dark. What light there was, coming through the black branches above, shone on the wet flagstones and helped her to avoid the lethal slippy patches. It wouldn't be the first time she'd fallen flat on her backside going down there. And that was hardly conducive to romance.

The picture was due to start at three, but there was already a queue at the Albert. Just as well she had the tickets. No Harry yet. She'd spot him right away if he was there. Only a motley line of lads in various uniforms, some with an amorous look in their eyes, arm round a Kirkwall lass dressed to the nines.

Eva joined the queue, keeping as close to the inside as she could. The walls have eyes in Orkney. There was always somebody who would spot you. Depending on who it was, you could be in big trouble at the school, even bigger trouble at home. But she'd take her chances.

She was glad she'd thought to wear her blue blouse, the one Harry admired the day last summer they went to Stenness.

'That blouse is the exact same colour as them flowers,'

he said. He was pointing to the wild lupins falling in drifts from where they were sitting at the top of the hill, right down to the road below, nearly as far as the two lochs and the Standing Stones. 'And them flowers are the exact same colour as your peepers.'

He kissed her then, so softly on the lips, her bones melted. His brown eyes locked onto her lupin-blues and mesmerised her so completely with their amber flecks, it wasn't till she felt cool air on her bare skin that she realised he was quietly unbuttoning her blouse.

She came to, flustered, pulled away, turned to button herself up. When she faced him again, he was lighting a fag and looking down towards the Ring of Brodgar.

'What manner of man,' he said, 'could've hauled them stones for miles and miles to that bit of land – that narrow strip there – and hoisted them to attention in a perfect circle? Some bleedin military operation, that was!' He looked to her for a response and she could find no trace of disappointment in his voice or his gaze. She said nothing. It had never once occurred to her that real men had raised those stones. They were just there. They always had been. He put his arm across her shoulder and traced circles round the distant stones with his cigarette.

'Ello, darlin!' It was Harry's friend Tommy, grinning ear to ear, his beret folded neatly under his khaki shoulder strap. "Arry's just coming. 'E's parking the truck. Blimey!

Should've known there'd be a crowd for Bogey!' Eva looked round. The queue stretched right up Albert Street to the corner of Castle Street now, all these folk lining up behind her, while her mind was in Stenness among the lupins. She could see Issy, hand in hand with Huw, a dozen or so back. It would be a full house for *Casablanca* again, even though it had been doing the rounds in Orkney over a week. Issy and her had already seen it in the Naval, but, oh, she was looking forward to seeing it with Harry.

A kiss is still a kiss ...

Her stomach flipped when he came into view. She'd nearly fallen out with Issy, arguing who was more handsome, Harry or Huw, but as far as she was concerned there was no contest. Harry was head and shoulders above them all! If it wasn't for his wonky tooth and his cockney voice, he would be a dead ringer for Gregory Peck, tall, dark hair, melting brown eyes, the lot.

'What you doing with my girl, Private Allan!' Harry stepped straight up to Tommy, snatched his hat out of his epaulette and hit him about the head with it. Tommy grabbed it back and they did a bit of pretend boxing, skipping about on the street with their fists up. Some of the men in the queue laughed and cheered. It would have made her laugh too, but Harry hadn't even glanced her way yet.

When they stopped, Tommy turned to her, 'What

d'you see in this clown? You're much too good for 'im.'

'Ah, but you'll miss me when I'm gone, Private Allan. How are you, my lovely?' He took Eva's arm, crooked his round it and looked at her properly for the first time. The queue started to move before she could reply and she longed to be quiet in the dark with him, away from this tomfoolery.

It was the first time she could remember people impatient to get through the Pathe News. Somebody shouted, 'Bogey! Bogey!' and bits of flung paper lit up silver in the projectionist's beam, like the tiny planes caught high in the searchlights when everywhere else was pitch black. But the news went on and somebody shouted, 'Shut up, you lot. My brother's in France.' There was some shushing from the lasses then and it quietened down.

The film started at last with the big map of Africa, that funny casbah music, a few bars *de La Marseillaise* and Eva sitting happy in the dark with her hand in Harry's. She wished she looked like Ingrid Bergman. Harry squeezed her hand as if he knew. She squeezed his back.

Time was different at the flicks. You were somewhere else, away from school and home and Ma on at you to collect the eggs and walking in the rain and wind past the camp and the squaddies looking miserable in the mud and you having to get back home before the blackout. Bogey and Bergman were the best. She leaned against Harry's shoulder. Even from this angle there was no movie to touch it.

Half an hour before the end of the film, Captain Renault blew his whistle and the picture started to melt. Bogey and Bergman fizzled out. Numbers and symbols jumped on the white screen. Then the lights went up. Eva looked around, dazed. Everybody was stunned. She saw various couples low down in their seats, pulling their clothes together. Two rows in front, she thought she saw Huw buttoning his trousers, while Issy looked away, embarrassed. She turned to Harry. He was lighting up a fag and smiling. And then the shouting started.

'Oi! Wot's the game? Wot you playing at?'

Mr Sinclair, the manager came down the aisle, waving his hands above his head. He ran up the steps to the stage. The curtain came down behind him, covering the bright screen and the flashing numbers.

'Ladies and gentlemen, ladies and gentlemen. Please.'

You could hardly hear him over the shouting. If it had just been an Orkney audience, you wouldn't have got that. But the boys had come in from Houton and Hatston and Grimsetter specially to see the film.

Mr Sinclair kept his hands up in front of him, as if he was expecting somebody to attack him.

'Ladies and gentlemen, I am very sorry, I regret to inform you that, in circumstances beyond our control, the last reel has not arrived from Lyness.'

There was a roar from the seats. Some people shouted they wanted their money back.

'But what I can say is, what I can say, we will do our utmost to bring the complete film to you in a few days, at no extra cost to those of you who have purchased tickets for today's showing.'

'Well,' said Harry, 'that's no good to me, is it, Private Allan?' Tommy leaned forward from the other side of Harry and looked at Eva.

'Ah, don't take it to heart, darlin. We know how it ends anyway.'

'Come on,' Harry said, 'let's get out of here.'

They got to the cafe before most of the rest of the audience had a chance to get out of the Albert. The bell tinkled when Tommy opened the door. He moved aside to let Eva go in first and said, 'Not exactly Rick's place, but it'll have to do. No gin, love, sorry. Chips all round, then?' It was warm inside and the windows were steamed up. She took off her coat.

'This is on me,' Harry said.'

'Blimey! Mr Bigtime.'

Eva sat at a table near the door and Tommy sat across from her. He looked serious for once.

'You all right now, love?'

'Of course,' Eva said. But she couldn't look him in the

eye. It was only a film. They could go again later.

Harry was leaning on the counter, chatting to Mrs Flett. By the looks of it, she had succumbed to his charms too. You never usually saw her smiling that much. But the bell jingled then, the door opened wide and a whole dose of folk crowded in, rubbing their hands and making for the counter. Eva was glad of the blast of cool air. She could feel her cheeks hot.

'Five minutes,' Harry said when he came over and sat down. 'Be ready in five minutes. Caught them on the hop in the chip department what with the film finishing early.'

He still wasn't looking at her and Tommy and him sat quiet. Harry took two cigarettes out of a packet, lit one, handed it to Tommy, then lit the other for himself and examined the glowing tip.

Mrs Flett came over with a covered dish and set it on the table. Harry looked up at her and smiled and winked. Eva could swear she blushed.

'Right,' said Tommy, 'who's for a chip?'

He lifted the cover and stopped. 'What's this?'

'What does it look like?' Harry said.

'Jesus Christ, Harry!' He looked at Eva and put the cover back on. He sat back in his chair and took a furious draw on his fag.

'It's a hill of beans, is what it is,' Harry said, and he pulled up the cover. Beans slid down the sides of a heaped stack of toast. Tomato sauce puddled on the plate. 'It's the last reel.'

Tommy got up and strode to the door. 'See you back at the base, you bastard.'

Harry had his head down, his hands on the table. He put his cigarette in the ashtray and took both of Eva's hands in his.

'No!' she jumped up. No, don't say it!' She had to pull before Harry would let go of her hands. 'No.' Couples at some of the other tables looked at them.

'Orders is orders, Eva,' Harry said. 'Nothing I can do.'

She took her coat from the back of the chair and hugged it over her shoulders, over her blue blouse.

'Don't be like that, Eva!'

She walked away from him. Through the jangle as she closed the door behind her she heard his last words.

'We'll always have Stenness!'

Writing The Last Reel
ALISON MILLER

Coincidentally, at the time I was asked to write a story for *Reel to Rattling Reel*, I was reading a 1944 diary kept by my teenage mother in wartime Orkney. My studious, serious, dux-of-the-school mother had entries every other day saying, 'Skinned school and went to the flicks.' Since the start of the war, cinemas had sprung up all over Orkney to entertain the thousands of troops stationed there. There were two in my small home town of Kirkwall, one just outside. It meant that many local residents enjoyed frequent visits to the cinema along with the troops. My story is entirely fictional, but draws on aspects of my mother's life. In February 1944, she went twice to see *Casablanca* and confided to her diary, 'Bogey sure can kiss!' From this short entry came the idea for the story.

Film Clips From The Murdo Macaulay Memorial Hall
DONALD S MURRAY

*On Wednesday night they rolled up the net, set poles aside,
packed rackets and shuttlecocks away, preparing for the
roll-down of the screen, setting out of chairs, beam of the
projector the next day.*

ON HER MAJESTY'S SECRET SERVICE

It's an ill wind that blows, perhaps,
a seagull between hydro poles,
leaving wings stretched between charged cables,
halting the projector as it rolls

out *Thunderball, You Only Live Twice.*
We saw Bond die two times one night:
his flight stalling on the volcano's edge;
the expiring, too, of his light

as he lay in an assassin's arms.
It wasn't that rare. Arrows would stall
and drop from view in Westerns.
Darkness fall with each squall

that blew the island's way.
There are some films that – for me –
have never reached a climax,
where both light and sound simply failed, fading fast
away.

On the croft, the cock's crow dispersing darkness,
declaring dawn; inside the hall, the rooster's call,
proclaiming darkness, the evening's diversions.

THE SPY WHO CAME IN FROM THE COLD

The title was a misnomer, for we sat in the chill
zipped up in our parkas, trusting we'd be heated by the
thrill
of car-chase and gun-battle, a bikini-wearing girl

rising like a siren from the waves. But none of that
occurred.
Instead we paid witness to a world
more monochrome than our own, all watchtowers,
security guards,

the only sirens signaling alarm when someone
clambered concrete

or leapt over Checkpoint Charlie. No wonder then our feet
grew restless, drumming the hall floor, seeking residual heat

and relieved when Richard went for a Burton, spotlights
sweeping across his corpse as he tumbled to the street.

Some nights a fog of voices squabbling over peat-banks,
roods of rocks where flocks might graze; other times a
mist of Capstan, single shaft slicing through the haze.

CULLODEN

The only time we heard words expressed
in our native tongue
were cries of distress
clansmen called out in *Culloden*

when redcoats jabbed bayonets
through plaid and philabeg;
the lamentations let loose
by dark silhouettes

who lost the battle
and its damned aftermath.
Their talk meant little to us,
for all our ancestors suffered the lash

of tawse and prohibition,
wooden bolt fastened round the neck.
Much easier to hunt Germans across moorland,
combat the evils of the KGB and SMERSH

than see ourselves in these defeated souls,
clans scattered and dispersed.

Going to the Flicks
DENISE BENNETT

We know we belong to the land
and the land we belong to is grand.
O.K.L.A.H.O.M.A – Oklahoma.
That was the first film I ever saw.
My neighbour Karen New bought the L.P.
and we crowded into her sitting room
to sing *Many a new day... de, de, de, de*

We called it going to the flicks then,
saved up our bobs and tanners
to sit in the cheap seats, Mum
raked up change for fares and sweets.
When Cliff Richard fluttered our hearts
we queued at the local Odeon, waited in the rain singing
We're all going on a summer holiday.

Later, it was the *Sound of Music* –
posh-dogs for one and six with a slick of mustard.
We yodelled all the way home.
I will always be *sixteen going on seventeen*.

Gritty stuff next. I snuck in underage to watch
Up the Junction – grew into Xs –
loved Alan Bates in *Far From the Madding Crowd*.

Then I fell for James Fox, saw *Thoroughly Modern Millie*
four times and bobbed my hair.

Years later I took my son to see
The Muppet Christmas Carol, Hook
and *Bambi* – that was a wet one!
Drip, drip, drip little April showers.
We both cried when Bambi's mum died.

I go to the senior cinema club now
with friends Pat and Jen on Wednesday afternoons –
there's an interval with free tea and biccies.
We sit and bitch about the script, go back
for more – *Mama Mia, Les Mis, La La Land…*
Sometimes we see a vintage film:
The Red Shoes, Passport to Pimlico,
the *Third Man* – *na, na, na, na, na,na, na.*
Professor Sue Harper from the University
gives us a lecture – a post-show chat.
I'm still unreeling my life through film,
still fourteen and *Singin' in the Rain.*

My Epic Hero
LEONIE MHARI AND ELINOR SCARTH

                        You are
            my   epic   hero.
          You are big enough on a big screen
        to   fill   my   face with   brawny   colour.
      Here,   I   can   rest   and   be   thankful
                              in your bright body.
      Yes, you are my epic hero.

   Harvest moon,
  the babber bear is growling, mind
  - ark at ee.
                          Listen, or you'll catch naen.
                              Clouds chanken by,
                      gien shade to yer muckle face.

    On   the   gurt   big,   big   screen,   down   the   cinemawl
     as   the   dimpsey makes way for the lectric night
       dinnum,   didn't we,
         project   our   hopes,   our   dreams?
           Will   you   carry   them   there   ideals
               into the darkness?
                      My   epic   hero.

Magnificent Obsession
TRICIA STAKES

The old Odeon on Renfield Street, Glasgow holds such a special place in my heart. I saw so many wonderful films there when I was growing up. The glamour of those technicolour movies was a far cry and a welcome break from our council flat in the East End of the city. Not just because of the magical films but because it was there I set eyes on my first love.

It was a December evening in 1975. I was an impressionable spotty teenager with little confidence, little pocket money and not many friends. As always, I had gone to the cinema with my mum and dad. When there was a new film in town in those days, everybody headed to the Odeon. I remember it like it was yesterday. It was a clear cold night and a strange almost electrical charge was in the air; the excited anticipation of the crowd waiting in line. We were right at the back. The queue was all the way around the corner and things were getting tense. There was no online booking then, you had to wait your turn. Tension was running high. I could hear a girl a couple of feet in front of us saying worriedly, "We're never going to get in, we're never going to get in". This was making me panic. It was making the people behind us panic too and those behind them. The panic spread like Chinese whispers. A large woman in a fur coat started scolding her husband, "This is all down to you, Harry. I told you we shouldn't have gone to the pub first but oh no, you always know best".

It wasn't unusual to be turned away from a full cinema back then. As we slowly moved forward, an old man suddenly appeared in front of the crowd. He was very drunk and holding out a tattered cap asking for money while singing "That's Amore". I just kept my eyes front, willing us through the glass doors and into the foyer. Slowly but surely, we got there. As we entered, a wave of warm air hit me and I thought, thank God, we made it!

After getting our tickets, Munchies and Mintola, we made our way to our seats. The lights dimmed and the advertisements and previews began with Pearl and Dean playing in the background. Even today that tune gives me a flutter of anticipation when I hear it. Finally, as I sat there in great expectation, the movie began. Duh, duh, Duh, duh, Duh, duh, duh, duh, duh. The menacing music reverberated around us and we all looked on in horror at the poor girl being thrashed from side to side in the cold dark water. From that first bite I was hooked, JAWS!

As crazy as it sounds, at that moment, I fell in love with a twenty-five-foot man-eating shark. I was obsessed. My every waking moment, thought and talk was of Jaws. I got everyone and anyone to come see it with me, my father three times, my mother two. I even persuaded friends in my class who were not even friends but mere acquaintances to come with me. Fourteen times in total I saw the film. Anything I could get my hands on that had to do with sharks, I begged, stole or borrowed. I went from being the quiet shy girl in class to SHARK GIRL. People I didn't even know would come up to me and give me articles and photos they had got from magazines and newspapers. Even Edward Lynes, the class bully.

It happened one day as I was coming out of the corner shop beside the school. I had just bought a Curly Wurly. I thought he was going to steal it off me, but instead he just thrust a folded-up bit of paper into my hand and said "HERE." I was totally confused. As I opened it, l saw it was a photo of a shark coming out of the water with its mouth open and its black eyes staring. I was speechless and almost overwhelmed. In that strange moment the thought crossed my mind to ask him if he wanted to come see the film with me. I was so determined to see the film again, but then I thought that would be a step too far. That would be like asking him on a date and I couldn't do that. He was a boy and a bully. And I, I was still painfully shy. The whole thing made my head sway and spin. So, I said thanks and we parted ways, never to speak again.

In a short space of time I had acquired a Jaws bag, Jaws T Shirt, Jaws stickers all over my school books and even Jaws knickers. Our neighbour down stairs, Betty, bought me them for my birthday. My mum and her were friends.

One day while making my way from my maths class to PE, I fell down the stairs. I say I fell but I was actually tripped up by my so-called friend, Isobel McCourt.

She was mad with me because I refused to sing "Paper Roses" with her at the Monday lunch-time folk club. She wanted me to sing because she knew I was rubbish and it made her sound better. But I had caught on to what she was up to so I told her no, in no uncertain terms.

The next minute I was lying at the bottom of the stairs. As I lay there face down on the floor, I could hear the chatter all around me. "Oh my god, someone's fallen down the stairs", I heard Isobel say, "How did that happen?"

I was so embarrassed. I just pretended to be unconscious in the hope people would leave me alone, but they didn't. I could hear two boys hovering above me discussing whether they should pick me up and carry me to the medical room. One said, "If we carry her there, we'll get out of going to maths". The other said, "No, she's too heavy".

Suddenly, Mr Henderson, the History teacher appeared from out of nowhere, wearing his jet-black school gown. He picked me up saying, "Are you alright? Where does it hurt?". As he did this, someone shouted,

"It's Shark Girl, she's flashing her Jaws pants". My embarrassment was lessened by the fact that I could see the jealous look on Isobel McCourt's face as the most handsome, most fancied teacher in school carried me in his arms along the corridor, his cloak billowing behind him.

Whenever I was asked what I wanted to be when I left school, I would reply with utter conviction, "A marine biologist specialising in great white sharks". This was despite the fact I couldn't swim. Since seeing the film, I had no intention of even dipping my toe in water. This even extended to the bath. After all, it wasn't beyond the realm of reality in my mind for a great white shark to get up through the plug hole and fit in a four-foot bath. I even wrote a song dedicated to my love. I asked Isobel to sing it with me at Monday folk club, but she told me to get lost.

"*Way out in the open sea, far, far below. There is one that we all know. Who, who is he? Jaws! He's the greatest he's the king of them all. He knows which way to go down below, he frightens and he terrifies us all. Jaws, Jaws, who is he? He is the king beneath the sea. Jaws, Jaws. Who is he? He frightens and he terrifies us all. He frightens and he terrifies us all.*

The months passed, the seasons came and went and

two years later to the very day, I found myself standing outside the Odeon once more. This time, however, I made sure my mum, dad and I were right at the front of the queue. On that cold rainy December night, from a galaxy far, far away came the UK release of "STAR WARS."

My love affair with Jaws was about to come to an abrupt end and another magnificent obsession begin.

5

GROWING UP WITH THE CINEMA

remembering which film
AONGHAS MACNEACAIL

1 in the beginning

can i remember the first
film i saw, exactly?

it came in a van,
and was set up in
our wee school dining room

the projector being aimed at
a whiteish screen on its shoogly stand
was made ready to purr, when,
reel to rattling reel, the story was spun

for our knock-kneed rows of
breaths held in, on backless benches,
bright trustful eyes alert to follow
where heroic figures rode, marched, crawled
in their perpetual wars
against cold jackboots, frowning red coats,
or bright feathered heads, that always rose
in minatory ranks along horizons
bearing bows and arrows, which were
met by six-guns spinning out
their raucous messengers of death

there was some lore about the 45
among the boys, feeding a jacobite ardour
against cold hanoverian, imagined heavy
broadsword against our chosen claymore,
shaped from air and ready for the kill

we performed our acts of valour
in the playground during dinner-break
before the hand-held bell, and
mr headmaster called us back to sit
on benches made of brick disguised
as wood – gnarled presbyterian wood

on which we'd, once a month, sit
watching all those flickering dissonances,
where death was possible without blood, or
excess demonstrations of agony or grief

it wasn't always john wayne,
and it wasn't only john wayne –
jack hawkins (who won the war
five times, on land and sea) spread his
stolid english frame across the screen
and the others, resonant in name and
narrative in face, whether under wide-
brimmed hat or metal helmet, filled our
sorbent minds with strutting dreams

so then, on torchlit journeys home, we

held those galloping reins, charged down
our yelling slopes, prepared to board a
veering ship, drove tanks on roads that led,

we knew, to all that stale old wallpaper we
might pretend was camouflage, but knew
was what surrounded us when homework
could not be postponed, bed beckoning

but can i remember the first – ?
can i say it shaped my life, or opened
any door i hadn't found in books?
(in reading which, i once was told,
the pictures are better)

and, as long as there was action
(what was given to the eye as action),
each mind in that dark room was taken
into butte or canyon, trench or rampart,
living through each moment as we rode
our gallop, or, being soldiers, waded
through dark sucking belgian mud, until
the final reel released us into usual rain

2 history lessons

when you meet mel gibson, he is
not as tall as brave-heart wallace,
while the tale he tells is taken from

old chronicles as unreliable as all
the weathers we have ever known,
or told, in these, our fickle islands,
but watch him stride through glen
and forest, sword in hand, you'll
take as real (not quite the same
as true) his telling of our hero's
bright scenario where weapons
carve their mortal arcs through
air, flesh, bone, lines of ancestry
executing what blind harry in his
acts and deeds (regarding what
was actual) declaimed, at vivid
but invented length – whereas
we search the scraps of archive,
record, anecdote, or other, which
might have been more regular
narrations that should give us an
approximate peopled landscape
where ancestors could walk their
grainy reels unedited, while those
whose voices are still heard may
ask for signals that, when versions
seem to contradict, we be allowed
to scratch a truth from under them

what the books expressed was less
such grand chimeras, their landmarks
chosen for our clean comprehension,

that good be understood, and sought

the spider in the cave was there,
giving bruce, in lieu of fact, a parable

then kidnapped by a master, we were
drawn through rocky perils between
factions (each with sight on other's
throat), across tangled heathers, into
hunger, sickness, bare survival, until
home, to feed on *parritch* and *small
ale*, but robert louis's *ailean breac*
was one of us, if outlaw, still a gael

and charlie was the bonnie prince
we took our turns to be, when
mealtime weathers let us go beyond
the playground fence –
though, later, as we read, we might
assess him less heroical (escapist,
not afraid to face the force of war)

3 in normal school

there were days we don't recall
as dull
though clouds were commonplace
and breezes bit fresh skin,
but sitting in our wooden rows,

eyes, ears and hungry hearts were
open to the words delivered to be
chalked on slates, then chanted
into memory – or else

and after school, some
stretches of the road were dark,
where moses with his tablets
leaned across the old bridge parapet,
repeating (with the river's descant hiss)
remember what you must remember,
there are ten dictations you must
always follow, knowing they will have
to have a fluent sabbath airing

was it because they were small
that jock and johnny (without
weapons) knew how to instil fear
as playground warriors – their fists
tied missiles aiming at your face

boy grows

with noddy left behind and then
outgrowing enid blyton's tides of
secret sevens, famous fives,
(escaping their escapes) is
stepping out from innocence

and reading
feeds a hunger for
the layered tale, where men
stride through the pages at
a steady and assuring pace –
it was like finding
flowers on the shelves

when captain john, our author, steered
heroic *biggles* into battle, we all
flew that flimsy plane together
(though we'd never seen a plane
in flight)

later, neville shute would engineer
a simple sense of what was possible
beyond the everyday

and fleming's *bond* was
all of us, impossibly

boy grows,
kicks ball (against a wall), until
it bounces badly

dock's the weed that heals
a nettle sting

there were cataracts and skerries

we were not supposed to know, except
in adult company (with rod and line)

and there were girls whose
silent beauty taught us hurt
(though unaware, as, whispering,
they shared the humour of
the sense that they were being watched)

a fragrance may revisit you
as, walking down an unfamiliar road,
a blossom ripens
in a gentle breeze,
inviting visitors to sip their nectar
to be stored as honey
(for the hard times)

4 now

what was aleppo's on the screen
(or choose your distant city,
according to the day)
though careful editing ensures
no blood is visible
while distant men accuse (no names)
the other – blame and bloodshed
tangled in a harness of twined rages
while the engaged and the innocent

lie cold, each pulse of expectation stilled

think back to how berlin was levelled,
london blitzed – we may reflect that rubble's
rubble, blood is blood, it shouldn't matter
whether shown in faded newsreel or hot
bulletin – brutality is in the gentlest soul,
if faced with lethal dark intent, the will to
live is dominant, and i might, therefore, kill

read the papers, watch tv, but how avoid
the need to blame, as if by marking *them*,
we demonstrate our right to sternly frown
at all the sieges, rude or unremitting, not
allowing what the mirror shows of history

read the papers, watch tv, and ask again,
how many young americans were killed
today, by gun or gun
(or, ride again, john wayne, john wayne)

age wears drapes   behind which hazy
memory can hide   but i can still recall
that flicker taking me,
        sat in a row of breaths held in,
to distant places   where we became
our ninety-minute cinematic living dream

dead flies make art because the artist sees

a story asking to be told and leaves it to
the viewing eye to parse
        don't say it's no mona lisa
nor a frozen still from *Dracula* – don't leave
the script to cogitate on chill mortality

walk out, and let the lilting dances of
bright butterfly and dragonfly amuse,
but listen to the music of the honeybee

D'Pictirs
ANNE HUNTLEY

The Symbister Hall was my first experience of film. The hall was just a peerie walk doon Rocky road, fae the Cruden cooncil hooses, where I lived. My sister, aulder than me by nine years, had been coaxed and cajoled by wir folk, into takin me wi her. Tarzan was on. I was obsessed wi animals and had been shargin at Mammy to let me go as soon as I heard it was comin.

The hall stood lik a shoebox lowin in the low hairst sun as we walked towards it; doon the ruckely hill. The boats at their moorings, cam inta sight, black silhouettes on the glimmering orange sea. Still at the simmer fshing the air wis rich wi the Saturday smoosk aa fried herring. There wis a chugging soond comin fae the hall, a good omen; the engine wis wirkin.

At the door Glibbie's Magnie took up the money. He had a sheeny bald head un roond broon glasses. Anidder Magnie wirked the projector, Peerie Magnie, his hair wis the sam colour as the sky ootside. The screen wis on the stage un any light left aa windows wis extinguished by blood red flannel curtains. I wanted to sit at the front; Wilma didno. The big lasses sat at the back and the peerie boys sat at the front. The hall's widden panelling echoed wi the sound of feet clip cloppin to the back or dartin te de front fur the best seats. Widden forms filled the space, backless eens afore the stage, just oogin wi boys. Boys rowlin aff; shot by Indians, boys hidin under fur a better aim at the cowboys and when the lights went oot boys shoutin, "IT'S A GRUELLY!".

The hall fell silent. I becam oblivious te everything aboot me except the blairin music un the screen flickerin un dan the huge red letters 'SHE' burst onta screen. I can mind readin the wird, 'She', so I must have been able to read but I wis still sleepin in the sam room as my parents so I was probably six years auld. I wis confused why did it no say TARZAN. I tried to believe it really wis Tarzan, de wir natives runnin in jungle vegetation but nae monkey, nae elephants, nae Jane. By the time Ursula Andres entered the blue flames for the second time and her glorious cheekbones became all dat wis left of her, I wis captivated. Tarzan could go swing!

I can't remember walkin hom or goin to bed but I couldn't get to sleep. This was the early sixties and we didno hae electricity. I went to bed lik Wee Wullie Winkie hadden a peerie paraffin lamp. Peerie lamps mak muckle shadows and I saw the blue flames growin ower the bedroom waa, ower the cupboard door, comin oot ahint the curtains. She who must be obeyed, inhabited my lamp, her skull appeared an disappeared in the sma yallow flicker on the bedside table. I started te tink aboot death an immortality. If whit happened a film meant naebody could live forever dan dat meant I wid dee tuy, someday I wid not exist. The terrible reality strak me, an I wis stiff wi fear, couldno move, a panic rose in me un I did the only thing I could, I yelled for Mammy. It wis Daddy it cam, un he sang me to sleep wi,

Shenandoah…

'I long to see you, away, we're bound away
Across the wide Missouri'

Memories of Cinema-Going
SANDY MARSHALL

I was an eleven-year-old boy back in 1960. My earliest cinema experiences had been in Airdrie. I was born and brought up in Calderbank, a village just outside town, and the Saturday afternoon screenings in either the New Cinema or the Pavilion were a great attraction to us kids. The films were screened typically to audiences of local schoolchildren, boys and girls of my own age group, and many of us travelling by bus from neighbouring villages. Being allowed in town, we were expected to be on our best behaviour; although sometimes, overwhelmed by excitement, we would spill out of the cinema after the show, recreating the action scenes in the street and on the bus on our way home.

During the summer holidays that year, I spent the month of July, with extended family members, staying in a remote farmhouse in Machrie on the Isle of Arran. Our location and facilities could be described as rather modest. We had no car; there were no restaurants or cafes and only a tiny post office about a half hour-walk away. The wild countryside and the nearby beaches however were a child's dream. These were the reasons why we had come here after all. It was with great surprise and absolute delight that I discovered a weekly visiting cinema which took place in the village hall on the outskirts of Shiskine, the closest village to us, about six miles distant. After a great deal of persuasion, my mother finally relented and gave permission for her young boy to go. With no public transport available, and with many misgivings, I was allowed to travel on an ancient bicycle hired from a nearby farmer.

When the date arrived, I set off with only a slight air of trepidation. The weather was absolutely faultless that evening and I actually felt quite proficient on the old bike. The single-track road was literally traffic free but to say that the road was hilly would be a gross understatement. There were lots of tough climbs ahead for me but these were compensated by the many exhilarating downhill stretches. This built up my excitement as I anticipated the films, and really made me feel quite self-assured. The show was scheduled to start on the evening at 7.30 and would end around 9.45. I arrived at the village hall with time to spare. I deposited the bike at the side of the hall, paid my admission and confidently went in.

Inside, the village hall had a kindly and welcoming feel about it. I remember the dust particles dancing in the air, illuminated by beams of warming light from the evening sun shining through the windows. The hall was packed and I could sense an almost tangible atmosphere of expectancy as a buzz of conversations filled the space. This seemed like a very significant occasion being held in such an improbable setting. The audience consisted mostly of holidaymakers from Blackwaterfoot, a small seaside village close by. Wooden chairs had been arranged in rows, with an additional two rows of wooden benches at the front for the smaller children. A screen had been set up on a small stage facing the audience and a projectionist was busy preparing the 16mm projector in readiness to start.

Before long, the doors were closed, the window curtains drawn and conversations faded to silence as the projector whirred into life.

The screening started with two silent black-and-white comedy short films, one starring Charlie Chaplin as a tramp and the other with the Keystone cops. These were followed by a newsreel and finally, the main feature, The Bulldog Breed, a comedy starring Norman Wisdom. Watching films in this locality and environment seemed almost surreal but the audience, myself included, thoroughly enjoyed all the films, although perhaps not so much the newsreel. The show in due course ended, it had been a real success, the lights were turned on and a thrilled audience showed its appreciation with much applause and cheering.

My excitement, however, was not over yet. We all made our way out of the hall. When I reached the outside steps, I was a bit shaken to see only a dim pool of light from a lamp above the door and the audience gradually fading into the blackness beyond. I felt quite abandoned, thinking of my journey home all alone in this darkness. I hastily retrieved my bike, took a deep breath and walked with it on to the road. The bike had no lights, so I had no other option but to go onwards into the darkness.

I was not a stranger to darkness but on this occasion, it seemed much more extreme than I had ever encountered. It was a warm summer night, but the moonless sky and the absence of stars provided only sufficient visibility to identify the faint outline of the surrounding hills. I could see nothing else except the twinkling lights from distant cottages.

As my eyes gradually grew accustomed to the darkness, however, I could just make out the indistinct outline of the hedges bordering the road, nothing else, not even the road. As I became absorbed in my predicament, all my senses rapidly became alert and the excitement of the films seen only moments ago were all but forgotten for the time being. This was a real excitement although not entirely a welcome one. With resolve, I eventually straddled the bike and slowly peddled into the darkness, positioning myself midway between the outline of the hedgerows on either side.

In retrospect, my journey back to the farmhouse was uneventful in terms of drama or fearful incidents. The ghostly apparitions, which eventually revealed themselves as sheep wandering on the road, were by far the scariest.

As I slowly progressed, I became more settled in my surroundings. I was no longer startled by the sounds made by birds and small animals as I disturbed them in my passing. I started to relish the smell of the surrounding earth and plants. I was completely absorbed in the nature of my environment.

On the uphill stretches I dismounted and walked, captivating the atmosphere. On downhill stretches I freewheeled with no concern of danger whatsoever, driven by a rising elation. Eventually I could see the farmhouse lights and in due course arrived safely to the relief of my mother.

I felt a slight melancholy on returning, but only because the excitement of the evening had come to an abrupt end. Relating my exploits to my parents on my return, however, provided great satisfaction and pride. The evening had turned out to be a real adventure for me on many levels, and had given me one of the most memorable and exciting episodes of my childhood.

By Example
LAURA TANSLEY

There is a photo from school with the six of us where the wind has picked up and our long blonde hair, in shades of mouse to platinum, streams out to the left like we're all the same, a shoal of Crucian carp in cahoots, and where one starts and the other ends is hard to tell. Our fixed smiles don't reveal but remind us that Katie could never keep secrets, Jane jumped too quickly on any just-broken-up-with boy and Sarah, whose mantra was *say it to my face*, told girls whose hair had been an endeavour since age six that it was time to grow up, but didn't prefer their new pixie cut, and the reason why the boys laughed when you played basketball was because you looked too butch. The moment means nothing except that it's something and we all nod along when we watch *Angus, Thongs and Perfect Snogging*, despite none of us knowing anyone around Alfrick that looked like Aaron Taylor-Johnson, and nights in Worcestershire were just as bad as the days our parents told us would be the greatest.

Learning How to Act
LAURA TANSLEY

The kids who lived on the cul-de-sac played a game called mini troops. With cocoa-powdered streaks on their faces they Commando'd the mostly car-free street with army rolls and improv IEDs made from rocks and plant pots. Simon had to use string and sticks because his parents promoted peace not Predator, which meant he saw potential guns everywhere, yes-and-ing every shaft shape, twitching every time he spied a trigger-looking Total Recall twig. I was less adept; all spit and ricochets *pew pew pew* hitting walls not bodies, my feeble finger gun no match for Meisner-made uzi rapid fire pushed from lips that knew how to speak the bullets. Maybe I should have worked on this, learned to make a *drr drr drr* or *doosh, chuck-chick, doosh*. But I couldn't commit and I'm pretty sure it's why now I can't voice conflict, still waiting for the perfect comeback two decades later when my tongue is caught round a man-made epoch.

BIOGRAPHIES

COMMISSIONED WRITERS

Christine De Luca writes in English and Shetlandic, her mother tongue. She was appointed Edinburgh's Makar for 2014-2017. Besides children's stories and one novel, she has had seven poetry collections and four bilingual volumes published (French, Italian, Icelandic and Norwegian). She's participated in many festivals here and abroad. Her poems have been selected four times for the Best Scottish Poems of the Year for the SPL online anthologies.

Aonghas MacNeacail Skyeman, born 1942. Native Gael for whom school was entirely English-medium (Gaelic taught as second language). Gaelic poetry has taken him from Japan to Vancouver (venues including the UN Building and the Capitol in Rome). Also writes in English, occasionally in Scots. Journalism and broadcasting helped feed the family.

Kevin MacNeil Born and raised on the Isle of Lewis, Kevin MacNeil is an internationally renowned, multi-award-winning writer. MacNeil has written novels, poetry, films, plays and short stories. His books include *The Brilliant & Forever*, *The Diary of Archie the Alpaca* and *Love and Zen in the Outer Hebrides*. He has edited important volumes by Iain Crichton Smith and Robert Louis Stevenson. MacNeil has performed and taught in many countries and is a Lecturer in Creative Writing at the University of Stirling.

Alison Miller, born and raised in Orkney, has recently returned. Since 2012 she has been Scottish Book Trust Reader in Residence at Orkney Library & Archive and Writer-Co-ordinator in Orkney for Scottish PEN's Many Voices project. Her novel *Demo*, published by Penguin, was shortlisted for the Saltire First Book Award. She has had fiction and poetry published in anthologies and stories broadcast on BBC Radio 4. As a member of the George Mackay Brown Fellowship, she compiled and edited *That Bright Lifting Tide: Twelve Orkney Writers*. Her work has appeared in *Writing the North*, Edinburgh University, *Between Islands*, An Lanntair, *Orkney Stoor*, *Speak for Yourself*, *Turangawaewae*, *Beuy* and Abersee Press.

Christie Williamson is a poet from Yell in Shetland who currently lives in Glasgow. His poems have appeared in various periodicals. His first pamphlet, *Arc o Möns* won the 2010 Callum Macdonald Memorial Award. His first collection, *Oo an Feddirs* was published by Luath Press in 2015.

CONTRIBUTORS

Denise Bennett has an MA in creative writing and teaches poetry workshops in community settings. Her work has been widely published. She has two full-length collections, *Planting the Snow Queen* and *Parachute Silk*, published by Oversteps Books and a pamphlet collection *Water Chits* published by Indigo Dreams.

Eleanor Capaldi is a writer of stories and scripts. They have been published by Bare Fiction, The Skinned Knee Collective, Mechanics Institute Review, and performed spoken word at festivals including Mugstock and Aye Write. Eleanor currently works in a museum. The objects haven't come to life yet, but there's still time.

Richard Clubley was born in East Yorkshire and studied biology at Brunel University. After teaching he retired to write about Scottish islands – books and magazine articles. Having explored the islands all his life, he moved to Orkney in 2017. They are beautiful and the warm, generous folk are not unlike those in Yorkshire. He feels right at home.

Georgina Coburn grew up in Perth, Western Australia and worked in Canada, the UK and Ireland before settling in the Highlands of Scotland in 2000. She is an art historian, freelance writer and critic, specialising in Visual Art, Film and Photography. www.georginacoburnarts.co.uk

Sam Elder Gates Sam is from Ayrshire. Forty years a music teacher, on his release he completed an MLitt in Theatre

History at Glasgow. Sam is now enjoying himself with a group from Yoker Community Campus making local safaris and sharing stories through writing, illustration, photography and a guid dose of Glesga banter.

Ruth Howell was born in Belfast. She studied geology and moved to Scotland over 30 years ago to work in oil exploration. She's now a writer and garden designer.
If she can't be in the cinema she'd prefer to be in the garden. Consequently, her great novel remains unfinished.

Anne Huntley The early sixties was a time of optimism and improvements in Shetland. This story is based on my recollections of the feeling of growing up at that time. I was born and continue to live in Shetland.

Patricia McCaw has published poems in a variety of journals, including the Poetry Society's *Poetry News*, *Gutter*, *South*, *Orbis*, *Northwords Now*, and *New Writing Scotland*. At the beginning of the year she was in the final four of Cinnamon Press's Debut Poetry Collection and Cinnamon Press is publishing a pamphlet by her at the beginning of 2019.

Donald McKenzie studied drawing and painting at Grays School of Art, Aberdeen followed by an MFA degree from Duncan of Jordanstone School of Art, Dundee. He has won awards for his short stories. His inspiration stems from his interest and connection to the Outer Hebrides. He lives in Inverness.

Sandy Marshall shares an apartment in the West End of Glasgow with his partner Helene, who is studying for a masters degree in film curation at Glasgow University. Sandy is 69 years of age and continues at present, to work as a mechanical engineering designer. He has no desire to retire but hopes, in the near future, to find a croft or cottage in the Highlands or Islands, where he can realise an ambition to produce pottery and ironwork.

Leonie Mhari recently graduated with distinction from the Masters in Landscape Architecture programme at Edinburgh College of Art. In 2016, she completed her PhD, 'Breaking old and new ground: a comparative study of coastal and inland naming in Berwickshire' in the School of Critical Studies at the University of Glasgow. Her poetry has been published in the Dangerous Women Project, Gutter, Raum, and Dactyl, and she won the Alastair Buchan Prize in 2015.

Marion F. Morrison was born on the island of Barra and grew up in Glasgow. She studied at the University of Glasgow gaining an MA and later on during her teaching career, an MLitt for research into Gàidhlig medium education. Marion writes poetry in English and Gàidhlig and her first collection is to be published later this year.

Donald S Murray is from Ness in Lewis and now a full-time writer living in Shetland. His latest book is 'The Dark Stuff – Stories from The Peatlands' (Bloomsbury) which was published in April. His new book – and first novel – 'As The Women Lay Dreaming', inspired by the effects of the Iolaire disaster of 1919 on his native Lewis, will appear in November from Saraband. He has also published a great deal of poetry, journalism and other forms of writing, most notably the Gaelic drama 'Sequamur' which was performed in London, Belfast and Ypres as well as much of Scotland.

Kay Ritchie grew up in Glasgow & Edinburgh, lived in London, Spain & Portugal, worked as a photographer & radio producer & has been published in *Black Middens, The Glad Rag, Shorelines, Making Waves, Treasures, Honest Error, Poets' Republic, Gutter,* and *Landfall.* She was mentored by Clydebuilt mentoring programme & has performed at several events.

Kirsty Rowley is a member of Deeside Writers creative writing group. She has had a couple of pieces performed in a local scratch night at The Lemon Tree in Aberdeen. She is currently working on a new play and regularly goes to the cinema to see films rated 12 and above.

Elinor Scarth is a landscape architect and lecturer at the University of Edinburgh. She was based in Paris where she managed a wide-reaching portfolio of landscape design projects, and has returned to Scotland to develop her personal practice. Conscientious of the processes which form and transform landscapes, Elinor aspires to develop devices, which allow us to observe, understand, and question the landscapes we inhabit. Projects aim to conceive radical transformations through modest means. Recent projects include the creation of in-situ works for the 'Ville et Champs' Festival in Geneva, Switzerland and Land Art Festival «au coeur des Méditerranées», Domaine du Rayol, Cap Negre, France.

David Sinclair was born on Flotta four years before it became a hive of war-time activity. Returning after National Service, jobs included: shopkeeper, sub-postmaster, postman, farmer, registrar, auxiliary coastguard, community councillor and short-story writer, mostly using humour and Orkney dialect to make a point.

Tricia Stakes has a BA honours Degree in Media Theory and Production from Paisley University and an Open Studies Certificate in Theatre Studies from the University of Strathclyde. She has had three plays produced and has been performing stand-up comedy in Glasgow and Edinburgh for the past two years.

Laura Tansley's writing has been published in a variety of places including *Butcher's Dog, Dream Pop Press, Lighthouse, Litro, New Writing Scotland, The Rialto, Southword, Tears in the Fence* and *Stand*. She is also co-editor of the collection 'Writing Creative Non-Fiction: Determining the Form'. She lives in Glasgow and tweets from @laura_tans.

Sylvia Anne Telfer International award-winning Scots poet and short-story writer, currently working on a collection of Scots poems and a book. She has been a court reporter, in-house publications manager, etc., and has worked in Africa, the Far East and Middle East, birthing a fascination for all cultures and a better understanding of other folk.

Ailsa Thom lives near Glasgow, enjoys travelling and is renovating a draughty house. Her two passions are writing and salsa dancing – but she has yet to find a way to combine the two. She has had short stories published in *Litro, Mslexia, McStorytellers, The Ghost Story*, and *Flash Fiction Magazine*.

Roseanne Watt is a poet, filmmaker and musician from Shetland. Roseanne was the winner of the 2015 Out-Spoken Prize for Poetry in Film, and runner-up in the 2018 Aesthetica Creative Writing Award. Her first collection, *Moder Dy*, won the 2018 Edwin Morgan Poetry Award.

EDITORS

Sarah Neely is a Senior Lecturer at the University of Stirling, where she teaches Film and Media. She is co-investigator for The Major Minor Cinema (www.hifilmguild.gla.ac.uk) and has led on the creative writing strand of the project, from which this anthology arises. Recent publications include an edited collection of poems and writings by the Orcadian filmmaker and poet, Margaret Tait (Carcanet, 2012) and *Between Categories: The Films of Margaret Tait – Portraits, Poetry, Sound and Place* (Peter Lang, 2016).

Nalini Paul is a poet based in Glasgow. Her first poetry pamphlet, *Skirlags* was shortlisted for the Callum Macdonald Memorial Award in 2010. She graduated with a PhD on Jean Rhys and postcolonial subjectivity in 2008 and has since developed her collaborative practice with actors, musicians, dancers and visual artists. In 2009-10 she was George Mackay Brown Writing Fellow in Orkney, which included working with archaeologists and the RSPB. Her poetic work in progress, *Beyond the Mud Walls* received a Tom McGrath Award and was showcased for Stellar Quines's Rehearsal Rooms at the Traverse, Edinburgh in 2016. In 2017 Nalini was a Robert Louis Stevenson Fellow in France. Soon after, she was commissioned by the Edinburgh International Book Festival and An Lanntair Arts to travel to Lewis and Kolkata as part of the 'New Passages' project (2017-18).
www.nalinipaul.com